A STUDY GUIDE

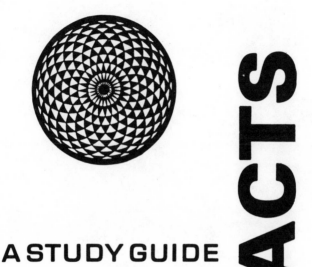

A STUDY GUIDE

ACTS

447

CURTIS VAUGHAN

ZONDERVAN
PUBLISHING HOUSE
OF THE ZONDERVAN CORPORATION
GRAND RAPIDS, MICHIGAN 49506

Printed in the United States of America

To
GLADYS

CONTENTS

Introduction

It would be difficult to overestimate the importance of the Book of Acts. Tertullian wrote of it: "Those who do not accept this volume of scripture can have nothing to do with the Holy Spirit, for they cannot know whether the Holy Spirit has yet been sent by the disciples; neither can they claim to be the Church, since they cannot prove when this body was established or where it was cradled" (quoted by Bruce, p. 25). Acts is the bridge which connects the gospels and the epistles, being the sequel of the former and providing the background for understanding the latter. It is in fact our primary authority for the history of the establishment and growth of early Christianity. "To it we owe almost all we know of the first spreading of Christianity in Syria and its arrival in Asia Minor and Europe; of the original gospel preached by the apostles; of the life and work of S. Peter and S. Stephen; and (apart from the notices in his epistles) of S. Paul" (Rackham, p. 2).

The *title* of Acts is stated differently in the various manuscripts. The better ones have either "Acts" (cf. ASV, NIV) or "Acts of the Apostles" (cf. KJV, RSV, NEB). The author probably did not give a title to his work. The book contains no detailed account of the work of any of the apostles except Peter and Paul. John is mentioned only on three occasions, and in each instance he simply appears as the companion of Peter and not as the doer of any special deed by himself. More space is devoted to Stephen and to Philip than to any of the other apostles. In light of this, it is thought by some that a more appropriate title might be "The Acts of the Ascended Lord." Others, alluding to the prominence of the Holy Spirit in the book, have suggested "The Acts (or Activity) of the Holy Spirit."

Referred to by name more than fifty times, the Holy Spirit is represented in Acts as empowering and directing the disciples in the accomplishment of all their work. Reference is made to the promise and gift of the Spirit (2:33, 38; 5:32; 8:18; 10:45; 15:8; 19:2); baptism in the Spirit (1:5; 11:16); fullness of the Spirit

(2:4; 4:8, 31; 6:3, 5; 7:55; 9:17; 11:24; 13:9, 52); effusion by the Spirit (2:17, 18, 33; 10:45); receiving the Spirit (2:38; 8:15, 17, 19; 19:2); speaking by the Spirit (1:2, 16; 2:4, 17, 18; 4:25, 31; 11:28; 21:4, 11; etc.); comfort of the Spirit (9:31); and so forth. Christ, we are told, gave commandment through the Holy Spirit (1:2); received of the Father the promise of the Spirit (2:33); was anointed with the Spirit (10:38); and has witness borne to Him by the Spirit (5:32). In addition, the Spirit is said to speak through Scripture (1:16; 4:25; 28:25); speak to the disciples (8:29; 10:19; 11:12; 13:2; 20:23; 21:4, 11); appoint to ministry (13:2; 20:28); equip for ministry (1:8; 6:3, 5); and direct in ministry (8:29, 39; 11:12; 13:4; 15:28; 16:6, 7; 21:4). Reference is made also to lying to the Spirit (5:3); trying the Spirit (5:9); and resisting the Spirit (7:51).

Acts, like several other New Testament books, is anonymous, but there is general agreement that its *author* was Luke. Ancient tradition, which is almost unanimous in ascribing the book to him, begins with the assertion of the Muratorian Fragment (c. A.D. 170) that Acts was "compiled in order by Luke the physician." Eusebius, famous church historian who flourished in the early part of the fourth century, gives this testimony: "Luke, by race a native of Antioch and by profession a physician, having associated mainly with Paul and having companied with the rest of the apostles less closely, has left us examples of that healing of souls which he acquired from them in two inspired books, The Gospel and the Acts of the Apostles."

Luke is mentioned by name in the New Testament in only three passages: Colossians 4:10-14; 2 Timothy 4:11; and Philemon 24. From the "we" sections of Acts we may learn something of his missionary activities (see discussion of 16:10).

The *date* of Acts is uncertain. It cannot have been written before about A.D. 63 (the probable date to which the last two verses bring the story), nor can it have been written later than Luke's lifetime. Bruce puts it before the outbreak of the Neronian persecution. Rackham argues convincingly for A.D. 63.

Numerous suggestions have been made concerning the *purpose* of Acts. Some, for example, see an apologetic intent behind the book, contending that it was written to show Roman favor to Paul (cf. Bruce pp. 20ff.). Lumby thinks the book was composed to give a history of the beginnings of Christianity, that is, to show how the Gospel was planted in various parts of the empire. Others understand the key to the purpose of Acts to be in its first verse, which suggests that Acts is a continuation of the story begun in the gospel of Luke. Scroggie accordingly states that the purpose of Acts was "to show that He who did and taught on earth is now doing and teaching from heaven" (p. 10).

The *plan* of the book is suggested by Acts 1:8. (See the discussion below.)

Acts covers a period of approximately thirty-three years (A.D. 30-63). At the beginning of this period Judea was governed by procurators, who had their permanent headquarters in Caesarea but sometimes took up temporary residence in Jerusalem. Pontius Pilate was procurator from A.D. 26 to 36. He was followed by Marcellus (36-37) and Marullus (37-41).

In A.D. 41 the procuratorial system was discontinued in Judea. In that year Claudius became emperor and shortly thereafter appointed Herod Agrippa I, grandson of Herod the Great, to rule over the area (see discussion of Acts 12). Upon the death of Herod Agrippa (A.D. 44), procurators were reinstated in Judea, and this condition continued until A.D. 66. Only two of these procurators are mentioned in Acts: Antonius Felix and Porcius Festus.

From A.D. 66 to 73 the Jews were in open revolt against Rome, and this revolt resulted in the destruction of Jerusalem (A.D. 70).

The world in which the Gospel was first preached was subject to the political authority of Rome. Its government was firm but in the main just, and much local freedom was granted. Rome preserved order, built good roads, and kept open communications between all parts of the empire.

The governing powers were the Senate and the emperor. The latter was supposed to be merely the highest public official, subject to the will of the people as voiced by the senate. But, as a matter of fact, his authority was practically absolute. The four emperors who ruled during the period covered by Acts were Tiberius (A.D. 14-37), Caligula (37-41), Claudius (41-54), and Nero (54-68).

Chronology of Acts. In the early chapters of Acts there are no fixed chronological data, but in the latter part of the book several definite notes of time appear (e.g., 11:26; 18:11; 19:8, 10; 20:6, 16, 31). There are two events of secular history mentioned in Acts which may be dated with certainty (the death of Herod Agrippa I [ch. 12] and the proconsulship of Gallio [ch. 18]), and these are of great importance in determining the overall chronology of the book. Arriving at an absolute chronology of Paul's life depends mainly on the date assigned to the accession of Festus to the office of procurator of Judea. Unfortunately, the scholars are not in agreement on this.

	A.D.	A.D.	A.D.	A.D.
Resurrection of Jesus	30[1]	30[2]	33[3]	29[4]
Pentecost	30	30	33	29
Conversion of Saul	35	34 or 35	34 or 35	32
Death of Herod Agrippa I	44	44	44	44
First missionary journey	46-48	48-49	46-47	46-47
Jerusalem Conference	50	49 or 50	48	48
Second missionary journey	51-53	begun 50	48-51	begun 48
Third missionary journey	54-58	begun 54	begun 53	begun 51
Paul's arrest in Jerusalem	58	58	59	55
Imprisonment at Caesarea	58-60	58-60	59-61	55-57
Accession of Festus as procurator	60	60	61	57
Roman imprisonment	61-63	61-63	62-64	58-60

[1]*Westminster Bible Dictionary.*
[2]*Zondervan Pictorial Bible Dictionary.*
[3]*New Bible Dictionary.*
[4]Rackham, *The Acts of the Apostles.*

CHAPTER 1

Final Ministry of Christ

(Acts 1:1-11)

Toward the close of his gospel Luke tells of Jesus' leading His disciples out to Bethany, where after blessing them "he parted from them, and was carried up into heaven" (24:50, 51, ASV). The disciples, he adds, "worshipped him, and returned to Jerusalem with great joy" (v. 52). The gospel closes with the summary statement that they "were continually in the temple, blessing God" (v. 53, ASV).

The first eleven verses of Acts, which overlap the concluding portion of the gospel, form the connecting link between the Acts and that book. The passage falls quite naturally into three divisions: verses 1-5, which form the preface; verses 6-8, which contain Christ's final commission to the disciples; and verses 9-11, which record the ascension of our Lord.

I. THE PREFACE (1:1-5).

These verses contain a summary of the "former treatise" (vv. 1, 2) and a statement of the nature of Christ's activity during the forty days between His resurrection and His ascension (vv. 3-5).

1. *A summary of Luke's gospel (vv. 1, 2).* "Former treatise," which is generally interpreted as a reference to the gospel of Luke, calls attention to its character as historical narrative. The Greek term *(logon)* was customarily used in this sense. Zenophon, for instance, employed it of the narrative portions of his *Anabasis*. Lake and Cadbury observe that the word was "a customary name for a division of a book which covered more than one roll of the papyrus" (p. 2). The use of "former" (lit., "first") has led some interpreters (e.g., Ramsay) to conjecture that Luke intended to write a third volume. This view, however, is rejected by most scholars.

The former treatise concerns "all that Jesus began both to do

13

and to teach" (v. 1b). It is debated whether any special significance is attached to the word "began." Lake and Cadbury, for example, take the negative view and assert that it implies no emphasis. It was, they say, simply a way of saying that the gospel contains the doings and teachings of Jesus "from the beginning." Haenchen calls it "a periphrasis for the finite verb" (p. 137). Others see in the word the notion that the gospel of Luke was a book of "beginnings," the suggestion being that Acts will set forth a record of what the risen Christ *continues* to do and to teach through his Spirit-led people. The gospel, says Walker, "contains an epitome of the Saviour's work on earth"; the Acts, "an epitome of His work from heaven" (p. 3).

"Until the day in which he was taken up" (v. 2a) defines the terminus of the gospel, and the point of beginning for Acts. The "commandment" (v. 2b) is interpreted by some as a reference to the so-called Great Commission (cf. Matt. 28:19, 20; Luke 24:47); others see it as pointing to the command to wait for the empowerment of the Spirit (Luke 24:49; Acts 1:4). The context may be general enough to include both.

The reference to Theophilus ("God-lover" or "loved of God") is another point of connection between Acts and Luke (cf. Luke 1:1-4). The language of both the gospel and Acts suggests that both volumes were dedicated to Theophilus. He was perhaps the one who defrayed the expense of writing and undertook to disseminate the two books. The descriptive title ("most excellent") used in the gospel leads some to think that Theophilus may have been a government official. The same honorific title is employed both of Felix (Acts 23:26; 24:3) and of Festus (Acts 26:25). Nothing more is known of Theophilus than what is told us in Luke 1:1-4 and the present passage.

2. *The period between the resurrection and the ascension (vv. 3-5).* Three things were urgently needed by the apostles if they were to accomplish the task assigned them by their Lord: (1) assurance that He was alive, (2) instruction, and (3) empowerment. The activity of the risen Christ was designed to meet these needs and thus to prepare the apostles for their mission to the world.

Assurance of the resurrection was given when Christ "shewed [lit., presented] himself alive" (v. 3).[1] (A similar expression is

---

[1]At least eleven appearances of our Lord following His resurrection are recorded in the Scriptures. There may have been others that were not recorded. Those which are mentioned are as follows: to Mary Magdalene (John 20:11-18; Mark 16:9-11); to the other women who went to the sepulchre (Matt. 28:9); to Peter (Luke 24:34; 1 Cor. 15:5); to the two on the road to Emmaus (Luke 24:13-35; Mark 16:12); to the eleven in the evening, Thomas being

found in Acts 9:41, where it is said that Peter "presented [Dorcas] alive.") This Jesus did "by many proofs" (v. 3). The Greek word, an unusual one which occurs nowhere else in the New Testament, denotes a demonstrative proof or an evidence manifest to the senses. By such proofs the risen Lord gave the apostles convincing evidence of His identity and of the reality of His resurrection from the dead. They were of such nature as to guard against the thought that the disciples were victims of a delusion.

The appearances, we are told, ocurred over the space of "forty days." This is the only place in Scripture which defines the length of time which lapsed between the resurrection and the ascension. The suggestion made by the text is that the appearances were given from time to time during the space of forty days; that is to say, the risen Lord was not constantly seen by the disciples as He was before His passion. These appearances were not mere optical illusions but miraculous manifestations of the person of Christ.

During the forty-day period Christ taught His disciples "the things concerning the kingdom of God" (v. 3b, ASV). We know, in addition, that He opened the Scriptures to His disciples, explaining to them the necessity of His death and resurrection (Luke 24:46); that He commissioned them to preach repentance and remission of sins among all nations (Luke 24:47; cf. Matt. 28:18-20); that He assured them of His spiritual presence (John 20:21-23; cf. Matt. 28:20); and that He charged them to wait for the empowerment of the Holy Spirit before beginning their work (Luke 24:49; Acts 1:4, 8).

The kingdom of God was not a new concept; it is found in the Old Testament, and the thought formed a prominent part of the preaching of John the Baptist. Essentially, it means the rule of God; in the present passage it must refer primarily to the messianic kingdom.

Verses 4 and 5 narrate an event occurring at one of the appearances of Jesus. Being assembled together with the disciples, He charged them not to leave Jerusalem until they had received the fulfillment of "the promise of the Father."

The commandment to "wait for" the promise often is lifted out of context and urged upon believers as a condition of receiving the fullness of the Spirit. This, however, reveals a misunderstanding

---

absent (John 20:19-24); to the eleven, Thomas being present, one week later (John 20:25-29; Mark 16:14-18); to the seven apostles by the Sea of Galilee (John 21:1-24); to five hundred disciples on a hill in Galilee (Matt. 28:16-20; 1 Cor. 15:6); to James (1 Cor. 15:7); to the apostles at Jerusalem (1 Cor. 15:7); and near Bethany at the ascension (Acts 1:6-11; Mark 16:19; Luke 24:50, 51).

of the passage. The stress is on the words "in Jerusalem." The charge then does not concern spiritual preparation but geographical direction.

The promise, which concerns the gift of the Holy Spirit, is described in three ways: *First,* it is "the promise of the Father" (cf. Luke 24:49; "the gift my Father promised", NIV). The phrase suggests that there is something special about this promise. It was originally given in Joel 2:28ff. and was reiterated by both John the Baptist (cf. Matt. 3:11; Mark 1:8, etc.) and by Jesus (cf. John 14:16, 26, etc.), but its ultimate source is in the Father. That is, it proceeds from Him. *Second,* it finds its realization in a baptism in (with) the Holy Spirit. References to being baptized in, with, or by the Spirit are found in the four accounts of John's testimony to Jesus (Matt. 3:11; Mark 1:8; Luke 3:16; John 1:33); in the present passage; in Acts 11:16, where Peter simply quotes this statement of Jesus; and in 1 Corinthians 12:13, which affirms that all Christians are baptized in or by the Spirit. The imagery of baptism suggests, among other things, abundant supply. *Third,* the fulfillment of the promise is at hand: the disciples would be baptized in the Holy Spirit "not many days hence," that is, within the next few days. The inference to be drawn is that the promise would find its fulfillment in the experience at Pentecost.

II. THE FINAL COMMISSION (1:6-8).

It is widely thought that the commission of Matthew 28 was given at the ascension and that other commissions found in Mark, Luke, and Acts are only variant reports of that. In reality, the commission was given on different occasions and to different groups. The passage before us appears to be the only record of the ascension commission.

The question asked by the disciples — "Lord, dost thou at this time restore again the kingdom to Israel?" — reflects their nationalistic feelings and thoughts. Since 63 B.C. their land had been under the dominion of Rome, and for more than six hundred years the Israelites had known no real independence. The disciples fully expected Jesus to effect a restoration of Israel's political sovereignty. They wondered if it was "at this time" that He would do it.

Jesus' reply was in two parts. In the first (v. 7) He asserted that it was not their business "to know times or seasons" (ASV). The Greek word for "times" is quantitative, denoting something like the English "era"; that is, it marks the general period of an event. The latter word speaks of the precise time of an occurrence. The NIV has "the times or dates"; Montgomery, "times and occasions."

These, explains Jesus, the Father set (determined) by the exercise of His sovereign authority. It is implied that He reserves the knowledge of these decisions to Himself.

The second part of Jesus' answer (v. 8) contains both a promise and a command. The *promise* is of power (Gr., *dunamis),* that is, the dynamic needed for efficient service (cf. Luke 21:15). Three things are to be observed: (1) It was the Spirit's coming which was to bring this power (cf. v. 4; Luke 24:49). (2) The power was to be for a specific purpose: witnessing. (3) The promise of power was for all the disciples, and it was unconditional.

The *command,* given in the words "Ye shall be my witnesses . . . ," is a reminder to the disciples that they are sent into the world not to make predictions about the future (cf. v. 7) but to bear witness[2] to Christ — to testify to what they had seen, heard, and known of Him. This, indeed, is the principal task of every Christian. Observe the following: (1) "My" witnesses, which reading is to be preferred over that of KJV, suggests the thought of *belonging* to Christ. It is implied, however, that they bear witness *to* Him. (2) "In Jerusalem, and in all Judaea and Samaria, and unto the uttermost part of the earth" (ASV) sets out the plan of Acts: witnessing in Jerusalem (chs. 1-7), in Judaea and Samaria (chs. 8-12), to the ends of the earth (chs. 13-28). (3) "The uttermost part of the earth" shows that Christ's parting concern was for the whole world. Moreover, the words presuppose that salvation is not restricted to Israel (cf. 9:15; 11:18; 28:28).

III. THE ASCENSION[3] (1:9-11).

Luke describes the ascension briefly in his gospel (24:51), but here a fuller account is given. The significance of the event may be summed up as follows: *First,* it is a necessary corollary of the resurrection. That is, it is the abiding proof that the resurrection of Jesus was more than a temporary resuscitation. To accept the bodily resurrection but deny the ascension, one must affirm either that Christ is still an inhabitant of earth or that He later died again. *Second,* it conveyed to the disciples the realization that the appearances, which had occurred at intervals over a period of forty days, were at an end. Thus it relieved their tension, put their minds at ease, so that, with the arrival of each new day, they did not

---

[2]The reference to witnessing strikes the keynote of the entire Book of Acts (cf. 1:22; 2:32; 3:15; 5:32; 10:39, 41; 13:31; 22:15; 26:16).
[3]Other references to the ascension are found in Ephesians 4:10; 1 Timothy 3:16; Hebrews 4:14; and 1 Peter 3:22. Passages such as Ephesians 1:20ff. and Colossians 3:1 presuppose the ascension. Jesus on three occasions made reference to His ascending to heaven — John 3:13; 6:62; 20:17.

wonder whether their Lord would again reveal Himself. *Third,* it suggested that Jesus was no longer to be perceived by physical sensation but by spiritual insight. *Fourth,* it was symbolic of His exaltation to the right hand of God. *Fifth,* it was indicative of His entrance upon His heavenly priesthood.

The chief features of Luke's narrative are its references to (1) the time — after Jesus' final discourse was finished (9a); (2) the place — "Olivet" (v. 12); (3) the witness of the disciples — "as they were looking" (9b; cf. 10a); (4) the cloud — a symbol of the divine presence and glory (v. 9c; cf. Exod. 14:19; Matt. 17:5 and parallels; 1 Tim. 3:16); and (5) the appearance of "two men . . . in white apparel" who promised that "this same Jesus . . . shall so come in like manner as ye have seen him go into heaven" (vv. 10b, 11). Some interpreters have identified the two men with Moses and Elijah (who were present on the Mount of Transfiguration), but most think of them as angels of God.

Three verbs are used to describe the Lord's ascent: "he was taken up" (i.e., lifted from the earth; v. 9b); "received" (i.e., caught up, enveloped, out of sight; v. 9b; "a cloud hid him from their sight," NIV); and "received up" (v. 11; "taken away," NEB) into heaven. The entire statement leaves the impression of calm grandeur.

FOR FURTHER STUDY

1. Read Luke 1:1-4 and Acts 1:1, 2.

2. Read Luke 24:13-53 and compare it with Acts 1:1-11.

3. Study and compare the "commissions" (Matt. 28:18, 19; Acts 1:8, etc.) of Christ to His people.

4. Using a work such as *The Zondervan Pictorial Bible Dictionary, The New Bible Dictionary* (Eerdmans), etc., study the following articles: Theophilus; Kingdom; Witness; Power; Great Commission; Ascension.

CHAPTER 2

Witness in Jerusalem

(Acts 1:12—8:3)

All that is recorded in verses 1-11 is in a sense preliminary to the major message of Acts. Having summarized the closing events of his gospel in those verses, Luke is now ready to unfold the thrilling story of the church's witness to Christ. It is presented, according to most interpreters, in three stages: Acts 1:12—8:3, the Jewish period; 8:4—12:25, the transitional period; and 13:1—28:31, the Gentile period. The first of these periods, which is our present concern, covers approximately three to five years, beginning about A.D. 29 or 30.

I. PENTECOST: THE WITNESS BEGUN (1:12—2:47).

The focal point of everything recorded in 1:12—2:47 is Pentecost. The passage divides itself naturally into three parts: (1) the prelude to Pentecost (1:12-26), (2) the day of Pentecost (2:1-41), and (3) the afterglow of Pentecost (2:42-47).

1. *The prelude to Pentecost (1:12-26).* This passage sketches the first of several "cameos" of life within the primitive Christian community. The tone is that of anticipation[1] of the promised advent of the Spirit. The account concerns (1) the return of the disciples to Jerusalem (vv. 12-14) and (2) the selection of one of their number to fill the place vacated by Judas (vv. 15-26).

(1) *The return to Jerusalem* (vv. 12-14). The Eleven, being Galileans, would not naturally have chosen Jerusalem as the center for their activities. It was the scene of their Lord's recent execution, and was hardly the safest place for them to be. Their return, then,

---

[1]These verses are often represented as describing the disciples' *preparation* for Pentecost, as though the coming of the Spirit were a reward for their striving. The facts do not support this interpretation. The disciples did not receive the Spirit because they sought Him, but because God promised to give Him (Acts 1:4, 5). Human desires and efforts had nothing to do with it.

19

must be thought of as an act of obedience to Christ's command. Jerusalem, in the plan of God, was to be the beginning point of the evangelization of the world; and they had been specifically instructed not to leave the city until the Spirit had come upon them (cf. v. 4).

"Mount Olivet," the place from which our Lord ascended to heaven, lies to the east of Jerusalem. "A sabbath day's journey," which is approximately three fifths of a mile, was the distance a Jew could lawfully travel on the Sabbath day. Luke's mention of the matter was perhaps intended to suggest that the ascension was virtually from within the city of Jerusalem. Upon returning to Jerusalem, the apostles "went up into the upper chamber" (v. 13, ASV). Rooms of this sort often served as places of assembly, study, and prayer, but occasionally they were rented as dwellings. That the apostles "were abiding" (v. 13, ASV) there suggests they were making this room their headquarters while they were in Jerusalem.

Some, in light of Luke 24:53, think the upper chamber was in the temple, but it is much more likely that it was in a private home. The passage in Luke implies no more than that the disciples daily frequented the Temple, observing especially the appointed hours of prayer. The use of the definite article *("the* upper chamber") has led many to think that some well-known room is referred to, perhaps the room which had been used for the last supper. It is conjectured that it was in the home of the mother of John Mark (cf. Acts 12:12).

Obviously the entire company anticipated the fulfillment of "the promise of the Father." Accordingly, they "all with one accord continued stedfastly in prayer" (v. 14a, ASV). "With one accord," which literally means "of the same mind or spirit," calls attention to their unanimity of purpose, feeling, and desire. The word is used ten times in Acts (2:46; 4:24; 5:12, etc.), but elsewhere in the New Testament only in Romans 15:16. The verb ("continued stedfastly") puts stress on the earnestness and intensity with which they gave themselves to prayer. It is an especially strong word, suggesting that they put themselves energetically into prayer. (Other occurrences of this word are in Mark 3:9; Acts 2:24; 10:7; Rom. 12:12; Col. 4:2.) That the group was moved to continuous prayer often is taken as an indication that they were seeking the promise of the Spirit. However, no reference is here made to the Spirit, and there is nothing to suggest that the Spirit's coming was conditional upon the disciples' prayers. A more probable view is that their earnest prayers were an indication that they had been profoundly moved by the ascension of Jesus and that they were anticipating, not making special preparation for, the advent of the Spirit. Luke 24:53 seems to suggest that praise was the dominant element of their prayer.

Joined with the apostles in this prayer were other persons: "the women," "Mary the mother of Jesus," and "his brethren" (v. 14b). Since the Greek does not have the definite article before "women," it may be better to render the phrase "with certain women." It is characteristic of Luke to call special attention to the place of women in the Christian movement.

(2) *The selection of a witness to the resurrection* (vv. 15-26). At some point within the ten days of waiting it was deemed wise to fill the breach made in the apostolic company by the defection of Judas. Some think it natural to suppose that this occurred toward the end of the period, but there is no way of knowing this.

The charge is sometimes made that the disciples acted rashly in selecting a successor to Judas and that they made a mistaken choice. Matthias, it is argued, is never mentioned again; Paul, they contend, was obviously God's choice to fill the apostolic vacancy. But it should be observed that (a) Paul never claimed to be Judas' replacement and apparently considered himself a special apostle with a special ministry. (b) Most of the apostles are not named again in the Book of Acts. Of that group, only Peter, James, and John are singled out for special notice, and the references to the latter two are quite incidental. (c) Luke gives no indication that he saw fault in the action which resulted in the selection of Matthias.

In considering the passage, one should take notice of the following: First, the role of Peter (v. 15). That he was spokesman for the group is what we would naturally expect, but, as has often been observed, his "primacy" did not qualify him to appoint Judas' successor. Second, the number of persons in the assembly (v. 15). The hundred and twenty in all likelihood were only a part of the total number of believers in the Jerusalem area, but there is no way of being certain of this. "Gathered together" (v. 15) translates a phrase which Bruce thinks has a quasi-technical sense, meaning something like "in church fellowship." Knowling sees it as emphasizing the unity of the group. Third, the explanation of the need for the selection of a successor (vv. 16-20). The essence of it is that the apostasy and death of Judas had been predicted in Scripture and therefore could not fail to happen. Lindsay calls this a reading of "the present condition of the apostolic company in the light of the word of God" (I, 44). Using the Scripture in this manner, Peter finds two things foretold: (a) that the traitor was to be one of the apostolic group ("numbered among us . . . obtained part of this ministry"; cf. Pss. 41:9; 109:2-5); (b) that the office from which he had been ejected was to be filled by another (v. 20). (Verses 18, 19 seem to be a parenthetical explanation inserted by Luke. The seeming contradiction between the statement of verse 19 and that of Matt. 27:5 may be resolved by combining the two statements and understanding Luke's account to supplement that of Matthew.) Fourth, the qualifications to be met (vv. 21, 22). Fifth, the method of selection (vv. 23-26). The two persons who qualified were chosen (v. 23). The group then engaged in prayer, asking God to indicate to them the man of His choice (vv. 24, 25). (They think of God as having already made the choice, and pray that He may reveal His choice to them.) Lots were cast (v. 26). This was a common Jewish way of determining the will of God (cf. Prov. 16:33). We may suppose that the names were written on stones, and the stones were placed in a container which was shaken until one of the stones fell out. This is the last time that this method of ascertaining the divine will is referred to in the Bible. Henceforth the disciples have the guidance of the Holy Spirit.

2. *The day of Pentecost (2:1-41).* That the apostolic witness should begin on the Day of Pentecost was profoundly appropriate. It was one of three great annual feasts — the others were Passover and Tabernacles — which all male Israelites were expected to attend in Jerusalem (Deut. 16:16). Some think it was the most popular feast of the Jewish year. Great crowds would therefore be present to hear the Gospel. Originally, Pentecost commemorated the completion of the grain harvest. It was therefore a fitting symbol of the great harvest of souls on that day.

In the Old Testament, Pentecost is called the "feast of weeks" (Exod. 34:22; Deut. 16:10), because it came seven weeks after the offering of the barley sheaf during the Passover season. It is also referred to as the feast of harvest (Exod. 23:16), the reason for which is obvious. Greek-speaking Jews gave the name "Pentecost" (meaning "fiftieth") because it came on the fiftieth day after the Passover sabbath. Ordinarily, Pentecost fell within the last two weeks of May.

(1) *The advent of the Spirit* (2:1-13). The coming of the Holy Spirit at Pentecost was an event of far-reaching importance. This is suggested not only by the prominence accorded it in Acts but by other things as well. The promise of the Spirit's advent, for instance, was given in the Old Testament (Joel 2:28ff.) and repeated by both John the Baptist (Matt. 3:11, 12) and Jesus (John 16:7; Luke 24:49; Acts 1:5, 8). Then, too, the disciples were charged not to leave Jerusalem until it had come to pass (Acts 1:4), and

their witness was not to begin until they had received the power consequent to that event (Acts 1:8). Only this could equip them for the work they were to do. D. L. Moody is reported to have said, "You might as well try to see without eyes, hear without ears, or breathe without lungs, as to try to live the Christian life without the Holy Spirit."

The advent of the Spirit, like the incarnation of God in Christ, had a once-for-all character. Pentecost, then, is as unrepeatable as the birth of Christ or as His death and resurrection. The event heralded the dawn of a new epoch, and the quality of life which it introduced is characteristic of the entire Christian age.

In 2:1-4 Luke carefully delineates the time, the circumstances, the manner, and the immediate effect of the Spirit's coming. The *time:* "when the day of Pentecost was fully come" (v. 1a). The ASV has "was now come"; NIV, "When the day of Pentecost came." A more literal rendering is: "when the day of Pentecost was being fulfilled." Some think the allusion is to the fact that the day, according to Jewish reckoning, had begun at the previous sunset, and thus in the early morning could not be said to be either fulfilled or past but could only be described as in the process of "being fulfilled" (cf. Knowling). Others (e.g., Hackett) suppose that the expression refers to the completing of the interval of time between Passover and Pentecost. Still others see in the words a reference to the arrival of God's appointed time for the advent of the Spirit (cf. Lenski).

The *circumstances:* "they [the 120] were all with one accord in one place" (v. 1b). "With one accord" translates a word not found in the best Greek texts. Instead, they have a similar word which means "together" (cf. ASV, RSV, NIV). "In one place" is probably a reference to the upper room (1:13), though there are some interpreters who think the disciples were assembled in one of the chambers of the temple courts. No special significance is attached to the fact that the disciples were "all together in one place," and we should not read into the statement any notion of meeting conditions for the bestowal of the Spirit.

The *manner* of the Spirit's coming is described in verses 2 and 3. The most striking features were the "sound" and the "tongues like as of fire" which accompanied the event. (Observe that the record does not assert that there was either wind or fire. "There was a noise and there were tongues; but there was neither felt blast nor felt burning. . . . The sound and the sight were the sensible garment of the spiritual visitation" [Lindsay, I, 48].) The "sound" filled all the house and resembled the noise made by the movement of a violent wind, "like the whirr of a tornado" (Robertson, p. 20). Wind often was used as a symbol of God's presence (2 Sam. 5:24; Ps. 104:3, etc.). Here it suggests not only the presence, but also the irresistible power of the divine Spirit. The "tongues" were flame-like in their appearance and brightness. At first they gave the appearance of one great mass of fire or cluster of flames; then they separated and were distributed in such a fashion that a flame-like tongue sat over the head of each of the assembled disciples. Fire, like wind, was a symbol of the divine presence (Exod. 3:2). Tongues, on this occasion, were perhaps symbolic of the conferring of divine power to utter the wonderful works of God. Both the sound and the sight were designed probably to produce a feeling of awe and an awareness of the momentous nature of the event about to transpire.

The *effect* of the Spirit's coming is described in verse 4. The central fact, and the greatest wonder, is that "they were all filled with the Holy Ghost" (v. 4a). This speaks of an inward experience of the divine presence. The word "all" is significant, showing that the experience was not confined to the apostles. They had received the Spirit on an earlier occasion (John 20:22), but that event was not the abiding and universal bestowal which had been promised.

To be "filled" with the Spirit is to receive as much of the Spirit as one can contain. Perhaps there is the added thought of being permeated by His presence and power, being brought under His gracious control. The term is a favorite one with Luke (cf. Luke 1:15, 41, 67; 4:1; Acts 4:8, 31; 6:3, 5; 7:55; 9:17; 11:24; 13:9, 52).

Though the Pentecostal experience was both a baptism (cf. 1:5) and a filling (2:4), we should distinguish between the baptism of the Spirit and the filling of the Spirit. The former is once for all; the latter may be repeated often (cf. 2:4; 4:8, 31; Eph. 5:18). Since Pentecost, believers have experienced the baptism of the Spirit at the time of conversion: "For by one Spirit we were all baptized into one body . . . and all were made to drink of one Spirit" (1 Cor. 12:13, RSV). Accordingly, nowhere in the New Testament are Christians commanded to be baptized with or by the Spirit. The filling is needed for effective service and Christ-like living, but nowhere in the Bible is it defined. Nor does the Bible tell us how to be filled, and it does not lay down any conditions for experiencing the filling. In Ephesians 5:18, however, we are commanded to be filled, and the verses following appear to describe the qualities which mark a Spirit-filled life.

As an accompaniment of their being filled with the Spirit, the disiples "began to speak with other tongues, as the Spirit gave them utterance" (v. 4b). The word for "utterance" (lit., "to utter") is an unusual one found in the New Testament only in Acts (cf. 2:14; 26:25). It seems to have been used of "eager, elevated, impassioned speech" (Robertson). In the Septuagint it is used only of the utterances of the prophets (e.g., Ezek. 19:9; Micah 5:12, etc.). "Tongues" refers here to foreign languages (cf. Acts 2:6, 8, 11) not previously spoken by the disciples. (The phenomenon of "tongues" is mentioned in only three other passages in the New Testament, Acts 10:46; 19:6; 1 Cor. 12-14). The reference in Mark 16:17 is part of a passage [vv. 9-20] thought generally by scholars to be a later addition to that gospel.)

Space will not permit a detailed discussion of the gift of tongues, but of the experience on the day of Pentecost the following should be observed: (a) The gift seems *not* to have been a permanent one intended as an aid to apostolic missionary work. No such power was really needed, for Greek was understood throughout the Roman world. (b) The gift was employed not for instruction but for praise, to utter "the wonderful works of God." It probably was accompanied by an ecstatic frame of mind, but it consisted of intelligible words understood without the aid of an interpreter. (This was not the case of tongues-speaking in Corinth.) (c) The gift was bestowed probably so as to arrest attention and serve as a sign indicative of the arrival of the new age. It made plain to the senses that God's Spirit had Himself descended in a new and unusual way.

Verses 5-13 tell of the effect of the Pentecostal phenomena upon the people in Jerusalem (both permanent residents and visitors). The "sound" (v. 6, ASV, RSV) which arrested their attention is thought by some to refer to the "sound . . . as of a rushing mighty wind" (v. 2); others understand the reference to be to the "utterance" of the disciples (v. 4). Bruce prefers the latter, but thinks there is no need to exclude the former. At any rate, the "multitude" — a favorite word of Luke, used in his writings twenty-five times — came together (v. 6). Their reaction generally was one of wonder and amazement. Observe the words which express this: "confounded" (v. 6), "amazed" (vv. 7, 12), "marvelled" (v. 7), "perplexed" (v. 12). Some, however, reacted differently: they mocked — the root of the Greek word means "a joke" — and accused the disciples of being "filled with new wine" (v. 13). According to Lindsay, the latter was sweet wine (lit., "sweet drink") made from the drip of the grapes before the clusters were trodden. Knowling also prefers the rendering "sweet wine," pointing out that the earliest vintage would not come until August. The "sweet wine" of the text was perhaps made, he explains, of "a specially sweet small grape" (p. 77). Bruce points out that "though the vintage of the current year was still some months off, there were ways and means of keeping wine sweet all the year round" (p. 65).

(2) *The preaching of Peter* (2:14-36). The speeches and sermons of Acts have occasioned considerable debate. Some, for instance, insist that they are the inventions of Luke and that he simply represents his characters as uttering them. Others look upon them as verbatim reports of what was actually said. Perhaps a mediating view is to be preferred. That is, we should see these addresses not as verbatim reports nor as fabrications, but as faithful accounts of the thought, spirit, and main content of what was said, recorded by Luke under the inspiration of the Spirit.

Peter seems always to have been spokesman for the apostolic band, and it is in that capacity that he addressed the assembled multitude. Many writers call attention to the remarkable change which had come over Peter since the time of his denials a few weeks earlier. Then he had denied with an oath that he even knew Jesus; now he stands forth and boldly proclaims Him to be Savior and Lord. The change can be accounted for only by the impact of the resurrection and the gift of the Holy Spirit. "With the eleven" (v. 14) shows that Matthias had taken his place in the apostolate. "Spake forth" (v. 15, ASV) translates the same word which is used in 2:4, and here as there it denotes elevated, impassioned speech.

The message may be divided into three parts: (a) verses 14-21, the introduction; (b) verses 22-35, the theme; and (c) verse 36, the conclusion.[2]

a. The *introduction* (vv. 14-21), which opens with a courteous address (v. 19b), takes the form of an explanation of the outpouring of the Spirit. The phenomena witnessed by the people could not be accounted for by attributing drunkenness to the disciples (v. 15). "It is but the third hour of the day" (9:00 A.M.), Peter declared. His allusion is to the fact that this was the hour of prayer, at which time the morning sacrifice was offered in the Temple. No decent Jew would drink wine or eat food before that time on a holy day such as Pentecost. The explanation of the remarkable occurrence of this day, then, had to be sought elsewhere.

---

[2]Another arrangement is as follows: (1) explanation of the Pentecostal phenomena (vv. 14-21); (2) a proclamation of the work of Jesus — His life, crucifixion, and resurrection (vv. 22-28); and (3) a confirmation and interpretation of His resurrection (vv. 29-36). This arrangement conforms to the structure of the passage, each part beginning with a personal address and closing with a quotation of Scripture.

Peter affirmed that it could be found in the prophecies of Joel (vv. 16-21).

The passage cited is Joel 2:28ff. Observe the following: (a) The "last days" (Acts 2:17), a common expression in the Old Testament (Isa. 2:2; Micah 4:1), denotes the days of Messianic blessing and judgment. Peter affirmed that these days had now arrived (cf. 1 Pet. 1:20; Heb. 1:2) and that the outpouring of the Spirit was evidence of it. The entire Christian era, therefore, is embraced in the term "last days." (b) God's Spirit is now poured forth upon "all flesh," without regard to sex (2:17b, c, 18) or age (2:17d, e). To Joel (as perhaps to Peter at this time) "all flesh" probably meant "all Jews." Read in light of God's whole redemptive plan (and subsequent happenings recorded in Acts), we must understand it to refer to all humanity — at least potentially. (c) "Prophesy" means to speak for God under the immediate inspiration of His Spirit. It may include prediction, but must not be confined to that. (d) The "wonders" of verses 19 and 20 may yet await fulfillment. They belong to the last days just as the experience of Pentecost, but perhaps they will find fulfillment at the *end* of the last days, that is, at the end of the Christian era. Some think the statements of verses 19 and 20 should be interpreted figuratively, and understand them to denote great and revolutionary changes introduced by the new age. We must not overlook the possibility that in Peter's mind the reference might have found fulfillment in the darkening of the sun at the crucifixion. (e) The "day of the Lord" (2:20) is an expression used in the Old Testament of a future period of God's manifested power, glory, and justice. It was thought of as a time of deliverance for God's people and as a time of judgment for His enemies. The New Testament identifies this day — sometimes called the day of the Lord, sometimes the day of God, sometimes simply "that day," etc. — with the day when Christ returns in power and glory for the judgment of His enemies and the consummation of His kingdom (cf. Rom. 2:5; 1 Cor. 3:13; Phil. 1:6; 2 Thess. 2:2ff.; 2 Pet. 3:7, 10, 12). (f) The divine purpose in this amazing manifestation of the Spirit is that "whosoever shall call on the name of the Lord shall be saved" (2:21). The redemptive work of Christ, crowned by Pentecost, opens up an age of salvation, and the offer is universal.

b. The *theme* of Peter's sermon (vv. 22-35) takes the form of a proclamation concerning Jesus of Nazareth. Beginning with the *man* Jesus (vv. 22) and closing with the ascended *Lord* (v. 34), it speaks of (a) the life and works of Jesus (v. 22), (b) His sacrificial death (v. 23), and (c) His resurrection (vv. 24-35).

(a) *The life and works of Jesus* (v. 22). We may assume that Luke has given only a summary statement of Peter's proclamation. In it four things are stressed: First, Jesus was a man "approved of God." The word rendered "approved" may suggest the ideas of demonstration, accreditation, appointment, and so on. In the present passage, Souter's *Lexicon* interprets it to mean "designated," "nominated," "appointed." The RSV translates it "attested"; Weymouth, "accredited"; Rotherham, "pointed out." In the papyri the word was used in the sense of proclaiming one's appointment to public office. Second, this approval (attestation, accreditation, etc.) was effected "by miracles and wonders and signs." The word for "miracles" (RSV: "mighty works") indicates manifestations of power. "Wonders," which is never used in the New Testament without the word "signs," calls attention to the impression made upon the witnesses. "Signs," a favorite word for miracles in John's gospel, speaks of the purpose served by Christ's mighty works. They were intended not merely to elicit the wonder of people but to direct their attention to God, the source of the miracles. The last two words ("wonders," "signs") are used together at least eight times in Acts. Third, these miraculous deeds were expressions of God's power working in and through Jesus. God did them "by him." Fourth, Peter's hearers knew all of this. "As ye yourselves [emphatic] know."

(b) *The death of Jesus* (v. 23) is represented from two points of view. On man's part, it was a brutal murder: "ye by the hands of lawless men did crucify and slay" (ASV). On God's side, it was part of an eternal plan for human redemption: "delivered up by the determinate counsel and foreknowledge of God" (ASV). Peter's intention was not to lessen the guilt of his audience; it was rather "to obviate a difficulty in the way of their believing that the Messiah could possibly be put to death," to show them "it was in the line of God's purpose that the Christ should pass through suffering into glory" (Lindsay, I, 54). The general sense is that man's wickedness in crucifying the Messiah could not thwart God's sovereign purpose. Indeed, man's very attempt to do so was used by God to accomplish His redemptive aims.

The Jews would understand "lawless men" to refer to the Roman soldiers, who, as Gentiles, were men without the (Mosaic) law. "Crucify," translating a word used only here in the New Testament, means "to fasten to (a cross)." "Determinate counsel" means fixed purpose. The TCNT renders it "definite plan"; NEB, "deliberate will." The Greek word for "foreknowledge" *(prognosis),* used in the New Testament only here and in 1 Peter 1:2, perhaps means more than "previous knowledge" (TCNT). Both here and in 1 Peter it has a connotation of "purpose." Moffatt translates the whole phrase: "in the predestined course of God's deliberate purpose."

(c) *The resurrection of Jesus* is presented with great fullness (vv. 24-35). The *fact* of the resurrection is affirmed in verse 24a: "whom God raised up, having loosed the pangs of death" (ASV). The meaning probably is that in raising Christ from the dead God released Him from death's agony (cf. Rieu, NASB, NIV). Some interpreters make much of the fact that the Greek word for "pangs" means "birth-pangs," concluding from this that the Scripture is portraying Christ's resurrection as a birth out of death. The imagery, they say, is that of death travailing with millions of dead people in her womb. When Christ was brought forth from the grave, the way was opened for others to follow. The first explanation is much simpler, and is to be preferred. (The Hebrew uses a word that means "cords" [cf. *Modern Language*]. In this, the imagery is that of death as a hunter catching and binding his victims with nooses and cords. Christ breaks the cords of death and rises victoriously from the grave.)

Three *proofs* of the resurrection are given: First, there is the proof of prophecy (vv. 25-31), the citation given (vv. 25-28) being a portion of Psalm 16. David gives his own experience (note "I," "my face," "my heart," "my flesh," etc.), but that experience is seen as typical of, and as having its larger fulfillment in, the Messiah (cf. v. 31). Verses 29-31 contain Peter's exposition of the Psalm. The thought is that the words cannot possibly apply to David himself, for he died and his tomb was still known to Peter's audience. Israel's renowned king was therefore speaking for God (v. 30a, "being . . . a prophet"), and his words have been fulfilled in the resurrection of Jesus (v. 31).

"In hope" (vv. 26, 31) means in hope of resurrection. "Hell" (v. 27) translates a word which denotes "Hades" (cf. ASV; lit., "the unseen [world]"). Here it refers either to death itself or to the abode of the dead. Goodspeed has "death"; Moffatt and NIV "the grave." The Greek word is not *gehenna,* which is regularly translated "hell." "Freely" (v. 29) means "boldly."

Second, there is the proof of eyewitness accounts (v. 32). The thought is, God raised Jesus from the dead, and of that fact the apostles are all witnesses.

Third, there is the proof of the Spirit (vv. 33-35). The pouring forth of the Holy Spirit, evidence of which the hearers had seen and heard (v. 34), was cited by Peter as the crowning proof that Christ had been raised from the dead and enthroned in heaven as exalted Messiah. "Exalted to the right hand of God, he has received from the Father the promised Holy Spirit, and has poured out what you now see and hear" (v. 33, NIV). Implied in Peter's words is the idea that the resurrection of Jesus was not a mere resuscitation, like that of Lazarus, the daughter of Jairus, or the son of the widow of Nain. He who was nailed to the cross now sits on the throne of the universe, alive forevermore. The words of Psalm 110:1 are quoted as finding their fulfillment in this triumphant event.

c. The *conclusion* of Peter's sermon (v. 36) is brief but powerful. The facts, supported by the witness of the apostles, the testimony of prophecy, and the manifestations of the Spirit, point to one conclusion: "So let the whole nation of Israel know beyond all doubt, that God has made him both Lord and Christ — this very Jesus whom you crucified" (TCNT). Lindsay observes: "In the Greek *ye crucified* is the last word of the sermon. He leaves that accusation to rankle in their hearts and bring home to them the enormity of their guilt"(I, 56).

(3) *The response of the people* (2:37-42). Peter's message electrified the assembled multitude. Their response, which was immediate, may be summed up as follows:

a. They were "pricked in their heart" (v. 37). The Greek verb is a strong one, and can be used to express emotional stress of various kinds. Here it suggests deep conviction. The literal meaning is "to pierce," "to stun," "to smite." Homer used it of horses pounding the earth with their hoofs. Rackham understands it here to mean "broken in heart" (p. 30); TCNT, "conscience-smitten." Beck renders it "they felt crushed." Thus broken and stunned by the enormity of their sin, the people cry out, "What must we do?" That is, now that we see that we have acted against God in our treatment of Jesus, what must we do to right ourselves with Him?

In verses 38 and 39 Peter answers their question. First, they are to "repent." The force of the tense is ingressive, expressing a note of urgency — do it now. The verb denotes an inward and complete change of mind which is rooted in the fear of God and sorrow for offenses committed against Him. Such a change of mind, of course, expresses itself not only in attitudes but also in conduct. In the New Testament the word "repent" occurs no fewer than thirty-four times, and was a keynote in the preaching of both John the Baptist and Jesus.

Second, Peter's hearers are to "be baptized."[3] This was a symbolic

---

[3]The Greek word for "baptized" is a third person imperative; the word for "repent," a second person imperative. This change from the more direct

act by which they expressed their repentance, confessed their faith in Christ, and openly identified themselves with His people. Most, if not all, of Peter's audience were familiar with John's baptism, required of all his converts as the outward and visible sign of their repentance.

Unlike John's baptism, the Christian rite is administered "in the name of Jesus Christ." The name of a person was thought of as an index to his character. To be baptized "in the name of Jesus Christ," then, is to acknowledge Him to be all that His name imports. Peter had challenged his audience to accept Jesus as Messiah and Lord. Their baptism in the name of Jesus Christ would be a public acknowledgement that they had done this. There may be an allusion to the fact that the person being baptized made an oral confession of Jesus as Messiah (cf. 22:16). The "name" may also suggest the notion of authority. The thought then would be: be baptized in acknowledgment of the authority of Jesus Christ.

Much debate has centered on the words "unto the remission of your sins." In interpreting them, at least two things should be kept in mind: One, they are to be connected not simply with "be baptized" but with both "repent" and "be baptized." That is to say, they enforce the entire appeal, not one part of it to the exclusion of the other. Bruce aptly remarks that "it is against the whole genius of Biblical religion to suppose that the outward rite had any value except in so far as it was accompanied by true repentance within" (p. 77). The same author calls attention to Acts 3:19, where the blotting out of the people's sins is represented as a direct consequence of their repenting and turning to God; no reference is made to baptism. Two, while never teaching that the act of baptism in itself effects a changed relation to God, the New Testament does reflect that the apostles regarded baptism and salvation as intimately connected. In fact, the thought of an unbaptized believer probably never entered their minds. The comment of Hovey about Peter's appeal is apropos: "He saw that the inward change and the ritual confession of it were so knit together by nature that it was enough for him to state them in their proper order and sequence. Repentance and the firstfruits of repentance were generally inseparable. The former could not be genuine without manifesting itself in the latter. And in the circumstances of that day a willingness to be baptized was no slight evidence of a new heart" (Hackett's commentary, p. 53).

The climactic promise concerns "the gift of the Holy Spirit."

_____

second person command to the less direct third person of "baptized" implies that Peter's basic and primary demand is for repentance.

This must not be confused with the *gifts* of the Spirit. The latter are special powers bestowed by the Spirit upon Christ's people to equip them for service (cf. 1 Cor. 12-14). The *gift* of the Spirit is the Spirit Himself. Believers receive this divine gift at the time of conversion.

b. "They that gladly received his word were baptized" (v. 41). To "receive" a message is to take it to one's heart, to accept it, to value it. The Greek word has in it the idea of welcoming (cf. Weymouth, *Modern Language*). To be "baptized" is to be immersed in water as an outward expression of changed attitudes, as an open confession of Jesus, and as a public declaration of identification with the followers of Jesus. The total number of those who thus responded was "about three thousand" — apparently more than had become followers of Jesus during the entire period of His public ministry (cf. John 14:12).

Verse 42 shows that the lives of the converts were turned in a new direction. "They continued stedfastly [the same word was used in 1:14] in the apostles' teaching and fellowship, in the breaking of bread and the prayers" (ASV). "They were regularly present at the teaching of the apostles and at the sharing of the offerings, as well as at the Breaking of the Bread and at the Prayers" (TCNT). Continuance in the apostles' teaching and fellowship revealed oneness of belief and oneness of spirit. The "breaking of bread" is probably a reference to the regular observance of the Lord's Supper, which at that time was part of an ordinary meal. "The prayers" is likely a reference to the prayers which formed part of the public worship of the Christian community.

3. *The afterglow of Pentecost (2:43-47).* Pentecost created a new fellowship. Verses 43-47 constitute a summary description of life within that fellowship. The paragraph covers a period of perhaps many months. Its teaching may be expressed in four statements:

(1) *The Christian fellowship was marked by reverence ("fear") and power ("wonders and signs")* (v. 43). In the statement that "fear [a feeling of awe, reverence] came upon every soul," the verb is in the imperfect tense, suggesting continuing action. The conviction of sin mentioned in verse 37 was "no momentary panic," writes Bruce; it "filled the people with a long-lasting sense of awe" (p. 80). This reverential fear was perhaps intensified by the "wonders and signs" (a comprehensive expression for miraculous works) performed by the apostles.

(2) *The Christian fellowship was marked by oneness and love* (vv. 44, 45). "All that believed were together [Weymouth, "kept together"; *Modern Language,* "held together"; Rieu, "lived as a

community"], and had all things common" (Rieu, "and shared everything"). This meant that they "sold their possessions [perhaps real estate] and goods [more portable property], and parted" the proceeds "to all men [i.e., the members of the community], as every man had need." All of the verbs in verses 44 and 45 are in the imperfect tense. Carver concludes from this that the reference is not to a general distribution of goods. "The sales of real estate and of personal property were made by the owners *from time to time* and the distribution was made on the basis of need *as the need developed*" (p. 35; italics mine).

(3) *The Christian fellowship was marked by worship and joy* (vv. 46, 47a). Three expressions characterize the disciples' worship: "daily" (ASV, "day by day"), suggesting that it was a regular practice; "with one accord" *(Modern Language,* "with a united purpose"; Rieu, "in unity of spirit"); and "in the temple." Acts 3:11 and 5:12 imply that the place in the Temple where they regularly gathered was Solomon's colonnade.

The "breaking bread" is thought by some interpreters to be a reference to eating the Lord's Supper (cf. 2:42); "did eat their meat" (ASV, "took their food"), a reference to ordinary meals. Bruce says "they took their fellowship meals in each other's homes and 'broke the bread' in accordance with their Master's ordinance" (p. 81). "From house to house" may mean "at home" (ASV) or "by households" (Bruce, p. 81). "With gladness and singleness of heart" may be understood to mean "with glad and generous hearts" (RSV).

(4) *The Christian fellowship was marked by continuous growth* (v. 47b). The Lord was adding (imperfect tense) daily to their number those who were being saved.

II. THE WITNESS OPPOSED (3:1—5:42).

The closing paragraph of chapter 2 gives an outlook of perhaps a year or more. The Spirit was mightily at work, pervading the entire Christian community with His presence, enabling the apostles to perform signs and wonders, and producing a quality of life among the believers which must have elicited a positive reaction from many people.

It is not surprising that under these circumstances opposition would soon surface. The section of Acts now to be considered records three occasions of such opposition: the healing of the lame man (3:1—4:35), the Spirit-filled fellowship of the church (4:36—5:11), and the growing power of the apostles (5:12-42).

1. *First occasion: the healing of the lame man (3:1—4:35)* This

passage tells of the first wave of opposition to the Christian movement. Instigated by the Sadducees (4:1), it led to the arrest of the two chief apostles and culminated in a solemn warning that they were no longer to speak or teach in the name of Jesus. The final outcome was a fresh filling of the Spirit on the part of the Christians, a strengthening of their fellowship, and an emboldening of their witness.

(1) *The miracle* (3:1-10). The healing of the lame man was probably not the first miracle to occur after Pentecost, but it was selected from the "many" (2:43) because it brought the apostles to the attention of the Jewish authorities and was the occasion for the first serious opposition. Before this time, the leaders of the people likely had not thought seriously about the new movement. Since Christians continued to attend the Temple, they were thought of as persons who, though entertaining fanatical ideas about the Messiah, were still adherents to Judaism. The tone of the passage suggests that several months, perhaps as much as a year, intervened between Pentecost and this miracle.

Verses 1-3 describe the *circumstances* of the miracle. It was at the ninth hour (3 P.M.) while Peter and John "were going up into the temple" (v. 1, ASV). The "ninth hour" was the time when the evening sacrifice was offered, and was observed as an hour of prayer (a time of public worship). "Were going up" (an imperfect tense) suggests that the apostles were ascending the steps leading up to the court of the Temple.

The man on whom the miracle was performed had been lame from birth. In 4:22 we are told that he was, at the time of the miracle, more than forty years old. "Was carried" (v. 2), an imperfect tense, means that the man was habitually carried to the Temple. In fact, he was "laid daily at the gate of the temple which is called Beautiful" (v. 2). The Beautiful Gate is not so named in any other known literature, and there are differences of opinion as to its location. It is thought by many that the reference is to what is elsewhere called Nicanor's Gate, which led from the Court of the Gentiles into the Court of the Women (cf. Bruce, p. 83; Haenchen, p. 198). Some would further identify Nicanor's Gate with the gate described by Josephus as composed chiefly of Corinthian bronze, and excelling all other gates in the Temple in the splendor of its appearance.

Luke's *account* of the miracle is in verses 4-7. Peter took the initiative and was spokesman. "Fastening his eyes upon him with John," he commanded the cripple to look at them (v. 4). "Fastening" denotes a fixed gaze. Williams: "Peter looked him straight in the eye." The man then gave the apostles his attention, thinking they were about to give him money. Then Peter, pointing out that he had neither silver or gold, offered the man something better: "In the name of Jesus Christ of Nazareth, walk" (v. 6, ASV). The "name of Jesus Christ" speaks here of the authority of Christ. The miracle was instantaneous: "immediately his feet and his ankle-bones received strength" (v. 7, ASV; "grew firm," *Modern Language*).

Veres 8-10 describe the *effect* of the miracle on the man (v. 8) and on the people who saw him (vv. 9, 10).

(2) *The message* (3:11-26). This section records Peter's explanation of the miracle to the wondering crowd. However, he goes beyond explanation, using this as an occasion for preaching Jesus and the resurrection. The message was delivered in "the porch [colonnade] that is called Solomon's" (v. 11). Located on the east side of the Court of the Gentiles, it was called Solomon's because it was built on a remnant of the foundation of the Temple erected by Solomon.

In studying this second recorded message of Peter, the reader should observe, among other things, its decidedly Jewish character — Stifler says the message is spiritual, "but its promises are largely Jewish" (p. 36); its numerous allusions to the Old Testament; the various titles and names for Jesus (Servant, Holy and Righteous One, etc.); the boldness and tenderness of the preacher; and the manner in which he sets the attitudes and actions of his audience (note emphatic "ye," vv. 13, 14) in contrast with the action of God. The message may be outlined as follows:

a. An explanation of the miracle (vv. 12-16). It is not to be accounted for by the personal power or godliness of the apostles (v. 12), but by the power of the risen Christ (vv. 13-16). Jesus is called God's "Servant" (v. 13, ASV), an allusion to the "servant" passages of Isaiah. He has been glorified, Peter explains, by the God of the patriarchs.

b. An appeal to the audience (vv. 17-26). Having declared to them in the preceding verses the greatness of their guilt, the apostle now explains to his hearers that in spite of the enormity of their sin they have hope of mercy from God. They acted "in ignorance" (v. 17, ASV); that is, they were not aware of the full criminality of their deed. Peter did not mean that this absolved them of their guilt; he was only suggesting that their ignorance made possible a merciful offer of forgiveness if they would repent (cf. 1 Tim. 1:13). Out of their crime, which was a fulfillment of the prophecies that the Messiah should suffer, God has provided redemption and forgiveness (vv. 17, 18). Peter's thought is echoed in the words of John Newton:

> . . . while His death my sin displays
> In all its blackest hue;
> Such is the mystery of grace,
> It seals my pardon too.

Verses 19-21 are a call for the audience to "repent . . . and turn again" (ASV). The two terms are very similar; perhaps the chief difference is that "repent" stresses a change in inward attitude and "turn again" emphasizes a change in outward conduct. This change in personal attitude and conduct is with a view to three things: (a) "that your sins may be blotted out" (v. 19; Weymouth, "cancelled"; TCNT, "wiped away"); (b) "that so there may come seasons of refreshing from the presence of the Lord" (v. 19, ASV), perhaps referring to rich and refreshing experiences following conversion; and (c) "that he may send the Christ who hath been appointed for you" (v. 20, ASV). This latter passage refers to the second coming of Jesus and suggests that the repentance of Peter's Jewish audience was part of the preparation for that event. Hackett explains that Peter mentioned the second coming in this manner "not because he would represent it as near in point of time, but because that event was always *near to the feelings and consciousness of the first believers.* . . . They lived with reference to his event. . . . It filled their circle of view; stood forth to their contemplations as the point of culminating interest in their own and the world's history; threw into comparative insignificance the present time, death, all intermediate events; and made them feel that the manifestation of Christ . . . was the grand object which they were to keep in view as the end of their toils . . ." (p. 62).

In verses 22-24 a solemn warning is sounded, the hearers being reminded that Moses, Samuel, and all the prophets that followed "foretold of these [Messianic] days" (cf. 1 Pet. 1:10-12). The sermon closes with a gracious promise of blessing (vv. 25, 26).

(3) *The arrest* (4:1-4). Peter's address — the closing words especially — stirred the authorities to action. "The priests, and the captain of the temple [i.e., the person who had charge of the temple guard], and the Sadducees" were "grieved" (ASV, "sore troubled"; TCNT, "much annoyed"; Weymouth, "highly incensed") about two things: (a) that such men as Peter and John, untrained in the rabbinic schools, were teaching the people (v. 2a) and (b) that they "proclaimed in Jesus" an actual instance of "resurrection from the dead" (v. 2b, ASV). The Sadducees denied the possibility of resurrection.

"They laid hands on" the apostles, but since it was already evening (too late for a trial) they jailed them overnight with the intention of disposing of their case the next day (v. 3). However, many of the people who had heard Peter's sermon became believers, bringing the total number of men alone — the Greek word is one meaning men in distinction from women — to about five thousand (v. 4). This is Luke's last reference to actual numbers.

(4) *The trial* (4:5-22). With the arrival of dawn there was a meeting of the Sanhedrin, the supreme court of the Jewish nation. This body, sometimes in the New Testament called "council" (Acts 5:21) or "estate of the elders" (Acts 22:5), consisted of its president (the chief priest) and seventy other members. Sometimes the Sanhedrin was referred to by some or all of the groups of which it was composed, as here: "rulers, and elders, and scribes" (v. 5). The "rulers" were perhaps Sadducees (the priestly party), who at this time were in the majority. "Elders" were heads of families; the term sometimes designated all of the Sanhedrin but seems here to be used in a more limited sense to refer to those members of the Sanhedrin who were not rulers or scribes. The "scribes," most of whom belonged to the Pharisaic party, were professional interpreters of the law. Luke's mention of the names of some of those present is an indication that he viewed this occasion as a very serious one. "Annas," senior high priest, and "Caiaphas," the reigning high priest, appear in the gospel records in connection with the trial of Jesus. "John" and "Alexander" are unknown. From the context it appears they were members of the high-priestly family.

The *defense of the apostles* is set forth in verses 7-12. According to custom, the accused were set in the midst of the Sanhedrin, who were probably seated in a semicircle. The apostles were asked, presumably by the president of the Council, "by what [kind of] power" of "in what name" they had performed the miracle (v. 7). (The pronoun "ye" is placed last in the Greek, giving to it a connotation of scorn and contempt. Bruce expresses this by rendering it "people like you.") The reference to "name" was intended to suggest that the lame man had been healed by some magical formula, such as exorcists used.

Peter, filled with the Spirit for the occasion,[4] made reply (v. 8). Observe the following: (a) the skill and ease of utterance with which he made his defense; (b) the stinging sarcasm in his opening remark (v. 9); (c) the boldness with which he charged the Council

---

[4]The Greek word for "filled" is an aorist passive participle and denotes "a special moment of inspiration" (Bruce, p. 99; cf. Acts 5:5, where "full" translates an adjective and denotes abiding character).

with murder (v. 10); and (d) the manner in which he turned the occasion into an opportunity for witnessing (vv. 11, 12).

The *decision of the court* is reported in verses 13-22. All those present "beheld [the Greek word suggests deliberate contemplation] the boldness[5] of Peter and John" and perceiving that they had received no formal training in the rabbinical schools, "kept on marvelling" (v. 13a). Moreover, they recognized something about the apostles — probably it was the power and boldness with which they spoke — which suggested a connection with Jesus (v. 13b). Being unable to deny the miracle and being in no position to dispute the claim of Peter and John that it was effected by the power of Jesus, they conferred among themselves as to what course of action they should take (vv. 14-16). It was decided to "threaten" the apostles and charge them "not to speak at all nor teach in the name of Jesus" (vv. 17, 18; NEB, "to refrain from all public speaking and teaching . . ."). Peter and John, however, replied that their duty was clear: "we cannot but speak the things which we saw and heard" (vv. 19, 20, ASV). After further threatening, the authorities dismissed the two men.

(5) *The sequel* (4:23-31). The apostles were faced with a dilemma. To go on with their work would amount to contempt of court; to remain silent was to disobey God. "They find their way walled up to heaven. They are in a strait from which there seems to be no human deliverance" (Stifler, p. 40). Recognizing their helplessness, they went to their fellow believers and appraised them of the situation (v. 23). Then they all, "with one accord" (TCNT, "moved by a common impulse"; Rieu, "in unity of spirit"; NEB, "as one man"; cf. 1:14; 2:46), laid the matter before God (v. 24a). This is the first recorded prayer meeting after Pentecost.

The *content* of their prayer is worthy of note. (a) They prayed to God as sovereign "Lord,"[6] the Creator of the whole universe, and as the ultimate authority behind sacred Scripture (vv. 24b, 25a). This was in line with their earlier declaration that they had to obey God, not men. (b) Their prayer was expressed in part in the language of Scripture, the fulfillment of which they saw in the events surrounding the death of Jesus (vv. 25b-28). (c) They prayed in submission to the will of God. They asked Him to look upon the threats which had been made, grant to them boldness to

---

[5]"Boldness" is the translation from a word whose literal meaning is "freedom of speech." Here the reference is to the forthrightness of the apostles.

[6]The Greek word is the one of which our word "despot" is a transliteration. It is used a total of ten times in the New Testament; of these, two references are to Christ (2 Peter 2:1; Jude 4) and three are to God (here, Luke 2:29; Rev. 6:10).

speak, and seal their witness by signs and wonders (vv. 29, 30; cf. 2:19, 22, 43).

The *results* of the prayer are given in verse 31: (a) "The place was shaken where they were assembled together." They had prayed to God as Lord of the universe; He answered in that character. (b) "They were all filled with the Holy Spirit" (ASV). It should be observed that this was *not* what the group prayed for. Their prayer was for boldness, etc.; God answered by giving to them a fresh filling of His Spirit. Nowhere in Acts is it said that anyone ever prayed to receive the Spirit. "We may be sure that it is proper, indeed desirable, for believers to ask for the Spirit continually (so Luke 11:13), but it is not necessary to do so in so many words in order to have the Spirit's presence or assistance.... We may be led, in fact, to believe from [Acts 4:31] that wherever there is the prayerful desire among Christians for the service of Christ there is the full gift of the Spirit" (F. D. Bruner, *A Theology of the Holy Spirit,* p. 171). This is the third reference in Acts to being filled with the Spirit (cf. 2:4; 4:8). From this it would appear that it is an experience which needs to be, and can be, repeated. (c) "They spake the word of God with boldness." "Spake" translates an imperfect tense: they continued to speak, etc. "Boldness" ("freedom of utterance," Rotherham; "fearless courage," Weymouth) appears here for the third time in the narrative (cf. 4: 13, 29).

2. *Second occasion: the Spirit-filled fellowship of the church (4:32—5:11).* The preceding section has recorded a wave of opposition against the Christian movement coming from without the fellowship. The present section narrates an instance of opposition from within. If Satan can't destroy the church in one way, he will try to do so in another way. Here he found two persons willing to be used by him: Ananias and Sapphira.

(1) *The background of their deed* (4:32-37). The originating circumstances of the sin of Ananias and Sapphira are found in (a) the general condition of the church (vv. 32-35) and (b) the noble example of Barnabas (vv. 36, 37).

a. The general condition of the church (vv. 32-35). This paragraph constitutes a sort of summary statement which reveals the inner life of the church (cf. 2:42-47). It is a picture of the church as the church ought to be: of one heart and soul (v. 32a), suggesting oneness and harmony; marked by a spirit of sharing (vv. 32b, 34, 35; cf. 2:43ff.); giving its witness in power (v. 33a); and enjoying the favor of God (v. 33b). It is often when things are going so well with God's people that the enemy comes in and seeks to subvert the work and destroy the fellowship.

b. The noble example of Barnabas (vv. 36, 37). Verses 34 and 35 speak of those who possessed lands and houses and sold them, placing the proceeds at the disposal of the apostles to be used as needs arose. Barnabas is mentioned (vv. 36, 37) as one example of those who from time to time did this. Perhaps he was singled out for special reference because his gift was especially significant. This is our introduction to Barnabas, a man of greatness in New Testament times. We are told of his tribal connections, that he was a native of Cyprus, and that "Barnabas" (meaning "son of encouragement")[7] was a nickname given him by the apostles.

(2) *The description of their deed* (5:1-11). Ananias and Sapphira are mentioned only in this passage. They were apparently members of the Jerusalem church. Their names, respectively, meant "God is gracious" and "beautiful."

Outwardly, it appeared that the deed of Ananias and Sapphira was just like that of Barnabas: they "sold a possession" and supposedly put the purchase price at the disposal of the apostles (vv. 1, 2). In reality, they "kept back part of the price" and brought only "a certain part" of it to the apostles. All of this was perfectly legitimate, as explained by Peter in verse 4a. Their sin consisted in their misrepresentation of the matter, pretending to give all but in fact giving only a part (cf. v. 8). This, in effect, was lying to the Holy Spirit (v. 3). "In attempting to deceive men," writes Stifler, they "were really insulting God" (p. 46). Viewed in another manner, the whole thing was "a deliberately conceived plan to see how far they could go in presuming upon the forbearance of the Spirit of God (for that is what is meant by 'trying' Him); and they had gone too far" (Bruce, p. 115; cf. v. 9). Love of money and love of praise lay at the root of their sin.

The punishment of their sin was unusually severe; indeed, some contend that it was unjustly severe. But we should bear in mind the nature of their sin (against the Holy Spirit), the newness of the Christian movement, and the imperative need for integrity if the work was to gain acceptance by the populace. Stifler comments that the judgment of Ananias and Sapphira was of the same character and for the same purpose as that meted out to Nadab and Abihu. "God would teach that nothing unhallowed can be admitted in the service of his house" (p. 44). We should note, in addition, the gravity of all sin — even our so-called "little sins."

---

[7]Significantly, practically every time Barnabas appears in the Book of Acts he is seen acting in the character of a man of encouragement.

The severe judgment upon this sin caused "great fear" (reverential awe) to come "upon the whole church, and upon all that heard these things" (v. 11, ASV). From this statement Bruce concludes "that many a member [of the community] had reason to tremble and say to himself, 'There, but for the grace of God, go I'" (p. 115; cf. 2 Tim. 2:19).

3. *Third occasion: the growing power of the apostles (5:12-42).* Now we come to the third expression of opposition to the Christian movement. The following general observations may be made: (1) This time it was directed against the entire apostolic company, not, as earlier, against just Peter and John. (2) This wave of opposition resulted in the infliction of bodily harm, and thus went beyond that of chapters 3 and 4 in intensity. (3) This, like the earlier, was instigated by the Sadducees, under the personal leadership of the high priest (v. 17). (4) It was occasioned by the growing power of the apostles (compare vv. 12-16 with vv. 17, 18). Accordingly, our disussion of the text revolves around the *evidences* (manifestations) of that power (vv. 12-16) and the *effect* of it (vv. 17-42).

(1) *The evidences of the apostles' power* (vv. 12-16). The close connection of this paragraph with the one which immediately precedes it should not be overlooked (note "and," the opening word of v. 12). The church, purged of evil, was now living in fear of God (v. 11). It is not surprising that under these conditions there was a resurgence of spiritual power. Carver remarks: "When the purity of the church and the obvious presence of the Lord in it make people afraid to join [cf. v. 13], then there is no way to prevent growth." (p. 57).

Three things in this paragraph point up the increase of spiritual power: One, miraculous demonstrations: "By the hands of the apostles were many signs and wonders wrought among the people" (v. 12a, ASV). "Were wrought," a translation of the imperfect tense, suggests that signs and wonders were from time to time (that is, repeatedly) wrought. So great were the manifestations of divine power that "they even carried out the sick into the streets, and laid them on beds and couches, that, as Peter came by, at the least his shadow might overshadow some one of them" (v. 15, ASV). Moreover, the news spread to the cities round about Jerusalem, and from them were brought "sick folk, and them that were vexed with unclean spirits: and they were healed every one" (v. 16, ASV).

No more remarkable exercise of miraculous healing power is recorded in Acts. Such power seems to have been vouchsafed to the apostles at this particular time to authenticate their preaching.

People are prone to look for such outward signs, and in the early days of Christianity the granting them gave evidence that the Christian movement had divine approval. But physical miracles were not given the preeminent place. Indeed, the apostles seem to have used them mainly as occasions for preaching Jesus. There are ample indications that not even the apostles could at will perform miracles. Paul, for instance, left Trophimus sick at Miletus (2 Tim. 4:20), and he prayed for, but did not receive, the removal of his "thorn in the flesh" (2 Cor. 12:7, 8).

Two, the fear and favor of unbelievers (v. 13). "The rest" is a reference to outsiders, perhaps the rulers of the people. "The people" denotes the populace as distinct from the rulers and other hostile outsiders.

Three, the growth of the church in numbers (v. 14).

(2) *The effect of this power* (vv. 17-42). The immediate effect was the arousal of *jealousy* in the hearts of the Sadducees. They had previously commanded these men not to speak or teach in the name of Jesus; but they continued to preach and perform miracles, and the movement kept growing faster and faster! (v. 17).

The next step was *the arrest* of the apostles. The Sadducees seized them and put them in the public prison (v. 18). The prison, however, was not secure enough. Verses 19-21 tell of the miraculous release of the apostles, effected by "an angel of the Lord" (i.e., a divine messenger). In accordance with the angel's instructions, they went to the temple area, and about daybreak began to teach "all the words of this Life" (ASV).

It was about this time that "the Council" (the Sanhedrin) and "all the senate" (perhaps the elders who were not members of the Sanhedrin) came together and "sent to the prison-house to have them brought up for arraignment" (v. 21b). It was soon discovered that the prisoners were not in the prison (vv. 22, 23); but eventually, after considerable consternation on the part of the authorities, someone reported to them that the apostles were teaching in the Temple (vv. 24, 25). Thereupon officers were dispatched to apprehend them, and they were brought, without violence, before the council (vv. 26, 27).

In the account of *the trial,* one should note: (a) The complaint of the high priest (v. 28). The apostles, he charged, were disregarding their earlier charge, going so far as to fill Jerusalem with their teaching; and were accusing the Sanhedrin of murdering "this man" (Jesus). (b) The testimony of the apostles (vv. 29-32). They reaffirmed their determination to obey God, not man (v. 29). They again charge the authorities with the murder of

Jesus and assert the fact of God's exaltation of Him (vv. 30, 31). Finally, they affirm that they are co-witnesses with the Holy Spirit to the truth of Christ's mission (v. 32). (c) The timely advice of Gamaliel (vv. 33-39). The authorities were "cut to the heart" ("were furious," Goodspeed; rage, not conviction, is the idea) when they heard the apostles' testimony (v. 33). Gamaliel, however, injected a word of caution. This man was the most learned and influential Jewish teacher of his day, grandson of the famous Hillel and teacher of Saul of Tarsus. Since he belonged to the Pharisaic minority in the Sanhedrin, perhaps he and his fellow Pharisees had enjoyed a measure of satisfaction in seeing the Sadducees frustrated by the work of the apostles. Gamaliel mentioned two men, doubtless well known to his fellow council members. Of one (Theudas) nothing else is known. The other (Judas) had led a revolt over the question of taxation in A.D. 6.

The Council accepted the advice of Gamaliel, and when they had flogged the apostles and charged them again "not to speak in the name of Jesus, [they] let them go" (v. 40, ASV). The apostles, however, rejoiced "that they were counted worthy to suffer dishonor for the Name" (v. 41, ASV; cf. Matt. 5:11). Furthermore, they did not cease "to teach and to preach Jesus as the Christ." Their witness was both constant ("every day") and consistent ("in the temple and at home") (v. 42, ASV).

III. THE WITNESS STRENGTHENED (6:1-7).

This section is introduced by a vague indication of time: "Now in these days" (ASV). The reference is to the period following the flogging of the apostles — the period in which they did not cease to teach and preach Jesus as the Christ (5:42). Just as the sin of Ananias and Sapphira came within a period of great spiritual revival (4:32—5:11), so the murmuring recorded in the present passage took place within another such period. The murmuring, however, is not the main point of this narrative. That was only the occasion for an official action of the church which resulted in the immediate strengthening and the ultimate extension of the Christian witness. Bruce speaks of this event as "a new and momentous advance in the community of the followers of Jesus" (p. 127). Some interpreters see chapter 6 as the beginning of the second major division of Acts.

The passage tells of the selection of seven men who were to assist the apostles in the distribution of food to needy members of the church. The service, then, was of a practical sort and did not extend to the "ministry of the word" (v. 4). These seven men are often popularly referred to as the first "deacons," but they are not so designated. In fact, the word "deacon" does not occur in the passage.[8] However, it is likely that the office of deacon, though not identified with that of "the Seven," grew out of the latter. As Hovey explains, "Their service was ... similar to that which the Seven were expected to render, and in principle the appointment of the Seven was the introduction of the diaconal service" (Hackett's commntary, p. 86). The only biblical passages in which deacons are explicitly mentioned are Philippians 1:1; 1 Timothy 3:8-12; and (perhaps) Romans 16:1, 2 (cf. RSV, Williams, NEB).

The situation which *occasioned* the selection of the Seven is set forth in verses 1 and 2. In short it was an emergency created by the continued growth in the number of the disciples. Because of that growth, it became increasingly difficult for the apostles to oversee the equitable distribution of food to the needy persons within the fellowship. Consequently, "there arose a murmuring of the Grecian Jews against the Hebrews, because their widows were neglected in the daily ministration" (v. 1, ASV). The complaint seems to have been well founded, but the neglect was not deliberate. The apostles were supervising all of the work (cf. 4:35, 36), and it had simply become too large a job for them to handle alone (cf. Jethro's advice to Moses, Exod. 18).

There is not complete agreement as to the identity of the "Grecian Jews" (Greek, *Helleniston),* though the majority of interpreters understand the reference to be to Greek-speaking Jews.[9] Many of these were Jews of the Dispersion, that is, natives of the Greco-Roman world. Lake and Cadbury admit that the reference may be to Greek-speaking Jews but suggest the possibility that the term may denote " 'Graecizing' Jews who are contrasted with the conservative party of the *Hebraios"* (p. 64). The "Hebrews" (Greek, *Hebraioi)* were mostly natives of Palestine and spoke Aramaic rather than Greek. There was tension throughout the Jewish world between the Hebrews and the Hellenists.

The *method* of selection is described in verses 3 and 4. The apostles specified the number to be chosen and the qualifications to be sought (v. 3), but the actual choice was left to the congregation. No special significance is to be attached to the number "seven"; presumably it was felt that this was the number needed to do the

---

[8]It is sometimes observed that the word for "ministration" (*diakonia,* v. 1) is built on the same root as the word for "deacon" (*diakonos).* This, however, is inconclusive since the word for the "ministry" of the word (v. 4) is the same as that for "ministration" in verse 1.

[9]The Greek word, *Hellenistes,* is built on a verb root, *Hellenizo,* which means "to speak Greek." The word which denotes "Greeks" (i.e., by race) is *Hellenas.*

work. The qualifications were moral and spiritual: a good reputation; fullness of the Spirit[10]; and wisdom, an indispensable quality of a competent administrator.

The *actual selection* of the Seven is reported in verses 5 and 6. Observe the following: (1) They were chosen by the people. (2) Their names are all Greek, suggesting that all (with the exception of Nicolaus [Nicolas, KJV], who was a Gentile proselyte) were Hellenists (the group from which the complaint came). (3) The listing of Stephen's name first and Philip's second points to the prominence of these men. Both of them ocupy a large place in the immediately following chapters. (4) The apostles, after prayer, "laid their hands upon them."

The imposition of hands was an Old Testament ritual used in the bestowal of a blessing (cf. Gen. 48:13ff.), to express identification (cf. Lev. 1:4; 3:2; 4:4, etc.), and for commissioning a successor (cf. Num. 27:23), and so on. In the New Testament it is seen as an act of benediction (Matt. 19:13), a sign of healing (Mark 5:23), a symbol of the impartation of the Spirit (Acts 8:13), and so forth. Bruce understands the laying on of hands here as formally associating the Seven with the apostles, "as their deputies to discharge a special duty. It did not," he explains, "impart the gift of the Spirit; the seven were already 'full of the Spirit' " (p. 130).

The *result* of this action was the general growth of the church (v. 7). "The word of God increased" (Weymouth: "God's word continued to spread"), "the number of the disciples multiplied in Jerusalem exceedingly" (ASV; TCNT: "rapidly"), "and a great company of the priests"[11] embraced the gospel.[12] The reference to the conversion of a great host of priests is a special indication of the growing influence of the Christian community. The Sadducees, who were essentially the priestly party, had been up to this time the principal opponents of the Christian movement.

IV. The Witness Sealed by the Blood of the First Martyr (6:8—8:3)

At this point Pentecost is five or six years in the past, and the Gospel has not yet been preached (so far as we know) outside of

---

[10]"Full" translates an adjective *(plereis)* and thus speaks of the abiding character of a Spirit-filled man. See note on 4:8.

[11]It is estimated that there were some 18,000 priests and Levites in Jesus' time, of whom 8,000 fell into the former category (cf. Haenchen, p. 264).

[12]This is one of several brief comments in Acts which summarize the progress of the Gospel. Others are 9:31; 12:24; 16:5; 19:20; 28:31. Some interpreters see these verses as keys to the structure of the book; and on this assumption they view Acts as made up of six "panels" of material, each covering approximately five years.

Jerusalem. The mention in verse 7 of the increased number of disciples in that city may have been intended to alert us to the fact that the time had now come when the Gospel was to break forth beyond the confines of the Holy City. "The church is now on the verge of a crisis. The appointment of the seven men to distribute the alms had an outcome surely not anticipated. It had started the church on its mission to evangelize the world" (Stifler, p. 58).

The key figure in this new direction of the Christian witness was Stephen, a man full of the Holy Spirit (v. 5), of faith (v. 5), of grace and power (v. 8). We see from verse 8 that his ministry became far more than a "serving tables" (v. 2); he "wrought great wonders and signs among the people" (ASV).

As we might expect, his work aroused a new round of opposition more bitter, more desperate, than any which preceded it. Three matters should be observed: (1) Heretofore the opposition to Christianity had been led by the Sadducees; now the Pharisees, who had been in the forefront of opposition to Jesus during His ministry, take the lead. Their persecution will be more determined than that of the Sadducees, for the point of contention now seems to be not just the matter of the resurrection but the introduction of an entirely new order which would strike at the very heart of Judaism. (2) The new wave of persecution began with the arrest and martyrdom of Stephen, but it was not confined to him (cf. 8:1b). (3) The great detail given to Stephen's ministry and martyrdom may be explained by (a) the fact that his was the first instance of martyrdom in the Christian movement, (b) his prominence in the Jerusalem church, and (c) his importance in the advance of the Gospel beyond the bounds of the Jewish nation.

1. *The arrest of Stephen (6:9-15)*. Stephen, probably a Grecian Jew, was associated with one of the synagogues frequented by Jews from the Dispersion. It is called "the Synagogue of Freedmen, comprising Cyrenians and Alexandrians and people from Cilicia and Asia" (v. 9, NEB).[13] The "Freedmen" were Jews who once had been slaves or were sons of former slaves. The mention of "people from Cilicia" suggests that Saul of Tarsus may have attended this synagogue.

The *reason* for Stephen's arrest lay in the fact that the persons who heard him speak were unable to "cope with his good practical sense and the spiritual power" with which he spoke (v. 10, Wil-

---

[13]It is debated whether this verse speaks of one synagogue (Bruce, Haenchen, et al.), two (Zahn), or five (Robertson). The version quoted above implies one.

liams). The *charge* brought against Stephen was blasphemy against Moses and God (v. 11). Doubtless Stephen had taught that the Mosaic customs were transitory and possibly had said something about the Christian salvation being for Gentiles as well as Jews. The false witnesses distorted his words and accused him of slandering both Moses and God. In pressing their charge against Stephen the authorities resorted to bribery (v. 11), mob psychology (v. 12), and falsehood (v. 13).

When the high priest asked, "Are these things so?" (7:1), he was in effect asking whether Stephen pleaded guilty or not guilty.

2. *The defense of Stephen (7:1-53).* Limitations of space do not permit a detailed analysis of this address. The following matters, however, should be carefully considered:

(1) *The importance of the address.* By virtue of the fact that it is the longest speech in Acts we must conclude that Luke considered it to be of far-reaching significance.

(2) *The object of the address.* In the strict sense, the speech is not a rebuttal of the charges brought against Stephen, but these charges always lie just beneath the surface of the argument. Lake and Cadbury call it "an impassioned attack on the conduct of the Jews" (p. 69). Bruce's remark is more to the point; he explains that the speech is "obviously not a speech for the defence in the forensic sense of the term. Such a speech as this," he adds, "was by no means calculated to secure an acquittal before the Sanhedrin. It is rather a defence of pure Christianity as God's appointed way of worship" (p. 141). Smith concludes that Stephen's address is important precisely because it is far more than a harangue against his judges or a personal apology (pp. 115, 116). Hackett sees a twofold object: "first, to show that the charge against [Stephen] rested on a false view of the Ancient Dispensation — not on his part, but on that of his accusers; and secondly, that the Jews, instead of manifesting a true zeal for the temple and the law in their opposition to the gospel, were again acting out the unbelieving, rebellious spirit which led their fathers so often to resist the will of God and reject his greatest favors" (p. 89). Hackett considers the latter idea to be the one uppermost in Stephen's mind.

Placed as it is in the Book of Acts, the speech is intended among other things, to prepare the reader for a witness to Christ which moves beyond Jerusalem and the Jews to include other people.

(3). *The arrangement of the address.* Although Stephen did not directly answer the charges brought against him, those charges are never far from his mind and his speech cannot be properly understood unless we keep them in mind. In effect his accusers charged him with saying that faith in Jesus implied the abandonment of temple worship and of the Mosaic ritual. In his defense he practically admits the charge and proceeds to justify his position. His argument takes the form of a historical narration. Verses 2-16 concentrate on the period of the patriarchs; verses 17-43 relate to the Mosaic period; verses 44-50 are concerned with the tabernacle and the Temple; and verses 51-53 are the application of the message.

According to Lindsay the address shows (a) that "the worship of Jehovah had not been confined in time past to Jerusalem, nor had His habitation been the temple only" and (b) that "the rulers of the people had continually made the same mistake as his accusers, had threatened and persecuted prophets who like himself had pointed out the true spiritual line of progress in the worship of their God, and had even slain the Messiah" (I, 88).

In developing the first of these points (God's worship not confined to Jerusalem), Stephen shows that God had been with Abraham in Mesopotamia, and that the patriarch had worshiped him there (vv. 2-8); with Jacob, Joseph, and Moses in Egypt, where they had worshiped him (vv. 9-24, 30-38); and with Israel in their wilderness wanderings, and had accepted their worship (vv. 44-46). To cap his argument, Stephen reminded the court that God does not dwell in houses made with hands. This, he pointed out, is evident from Solomon's prayer at the dedication of the Temple; in it he expressly declared that heaven is God's throne, the earth His footstool, and no one spot on earth the place of His rest (vv. 47-50).

The second point (God's purpose often missed by His people) is developed by pointing to *Joseph,* who, though rejected by his brethren, was God's appointed messenger (vv. 9-16, esp. v. 9); *Moses,* whose experience was the same (vv. 20-43, esp. vv. 35, 40); and *Jesus,* who, though not specifically named, is obviously referred to (vv. 51-53).[14]

---

[14]There are several discrepancies with the Old Testament record in Stephen's address. These, however, are for the most part "merely additions for which Stephen had the support of tradition or of literature not now accessible" (Carver, p. 69). For example, in verse 14 reference is made to "threescore and fifteen souls" as making up the household of Jacob. The Hebrew text of Genesis 46:27 and Exodus 1:5 reads seventy. Stephen was apparently following the Septuagint, which has seventy-five. See Bruce, p. 148, for fuller discussion.

The reference to Shechem in verse 16 also requires attention. Jacob was buried at Hebron, in the place bought by Abraham from Ephron (Gen. 23:16; 49:29ff.; 50:13). Joseph was buried at Shechem, in a place bought by Jacob from the sons of Hamor (Josh. 24:32). Bruce explains: "The two purchases of land are telescoped here in much the same way as two separate

3. *The execution of Stephen (7:54—8:3).* The reaction of the council to Stephen's address was vicious. They were "cut to the heart" ("were furious," NIV; the expression is the same as that used in 5:33) and "gnashed on him with their teeth" ("ground their teeth at him," NIV). Robertson comments that their conduct was like that of a pack of hungry, snarling wolves. Stephen, on the other hand, exhibited an air of calmness and peace. "Full of the Holy Spirit" (cf. 6:5), he "fixed his eyes intently on the heavens [TCNT; Williams: "looked right into heaven"] and saw the glory of God, and Jesus standing[15] on the right hand[16] of God" (v. 55, ASV). Then he said, "I can see heaven wide open [Weymouth] and the Son of man[17] standing on the right hand of God" (v. 56, ASV).

Those present could endure no more. They "yelled at the top of their voices" (Beck), "stopped their ears" (ASV), "and rushed[18] at him like one man" (Moffatt). Then having dragged him out of the city, they stoned him (v. 58a). Stoning ordinarily consisted in throwing the victim over a precipice, and rolling a heavy stone over his chest. "One witness threw him over head first, turned him over, and rolled a stone down. If this did not kill him the second witness rolled down another stone" (Lake and Cadbury, p. 85). "The witnesses," who by Mosaic law were required to cast the first stones (Deut. 17:7; Lev. 24:14; cf. John 8:7), laid aside the outer garments which they wore and put them in the keeping of "a young man named Saul" (v. 58b).[19] The scene must have been indelibly stamped on Saul's mind, and likely Luke was indebted to him for the details of this narrative.

Stephen's demeanor was in marked contrast to that of his oppo-

---

calls of Abraham are telescoped in v. 2 and two separate Pentateuchal quotations in v. 7" (p. 149).

[15]Only in this passage is Jesus described as standing at the right hand of God (here and v. 56). In every other place in the New Testament where similar reference is made to Jesus, He is described as sitting at the right hand of God.

[16]The "right hand" of a monarch was the place of highest privilege and authority.

[17]This messianic title, drawn from Daniel 7:13f., was a favorite of Jesus; and this is the only instance in the New Testament of its use by anyone but Jesus. Bruce considers this a fact "full of meaning." Manson calls its occurrence here "a remarkable fact . . . not to be undervalued or ignored. It is, on the face of it, a very distinct piece of evidence that, actually and historically, *Stephen grasped and asserted the more-than-Jewish-Messianic sense in which the office and significance of Jesus in religious history were to be understood.* . . . Stephen saw that the Messiah was on the throne of the universe" (quoted by Bruce, p. 166).

[18]The Greek word is the same as that used in Luke 8:33 of the swine rushing down the cliff when the demons came into them.

[19]The mention of the witnesses is an indication that the stoning of Stephen was an official action of the Sanhedrin (though carried out illegally), not a lynching by an unruly mob.

nents. Even as they stoned him he was "calling upon the Lord" to receive his spirit. Falling to his knees ("rising on his knees," Weymouth), he cried loudly, "Lord, do not hold this sin against them" (v. 60a, RSV). These words, reminiscent of our Lord's words on the cross, were Stephen's last, for having uttered them "he fell asleep" (v. 60b; Moffatt, "he slept the sleep of death"). "There are few more striking illustrations in Scripture of how Jesus' victory over death robbed it of its sting for his followers" (Winn, p. 61).

That Saul, introduced in 7:58, "was consenting unto" (8:1) Stephen's death does not necessarily prove that he was acting (voting) as a member of the Sanhedrin. It may only indicate that he was approving of the execution, as was shown by his caring for the garments of the witnesses (7:58b). Weymouth renders the statement: "And Saul fully approved of his murder."

There were immediate and far-reaching consequences of Stephen's death. "On that very day a great storm of persecution burst upon the Church in Jerusalem [Phillips]; and they were all scattered abroad throughout the regions of Judaea and Samaria, except the apostles" (8:1b, ASV). Thus began the fulfillment of the second part of the Lord's commission (1:8). The word for "scattered abroad" suggests the sowing of seed. "The blood of the martyrs" it has been said, "is the seed of the church."

It is not easy to explain why the apostles did not leave Jerusalem along with the other believers. Perhaps the authorities were reluctant to lay hands on them. Bruce suggests that the popular resentment was directed mainly at the Hellenists in the church.

Some think that believers were not even permitted to claim the body of Stephen for burial, making it necessary for "devout men" (i.e. pious Jews who were not Christians) to render this service. Others feel that though the term "devout men" is regularly used in the New Testament of pious Jews, it must here refer to Jewish Christians.

Verse 3 points up that Saul, a zealot for the traditions of his fathers (Gal. 1:13f.), was the prime mover in this new wave of persecution. He "began to devastate the Church" (TCNT), dragging men, even women, off to prison.

FOR FURTHER STUDY

1. Read Acts 1:12—8:3, watching for recurring words and phrases.

2. Make a list of all the personal names appearing in Acts 1:12—8:3 and list the passages in which each is found.

3. Using a concordance, make a list of references to the Holy Spirit in 1:12—8:3.

4. Make a list of the qualifications required in "the Seven" (ch. 6).

5. Read the articles in a Bible dictionary on: Miracles; Council (Sanhedrin); Gamaliel; Stephen; Hellenist; Grecian Jews; Deacon; etc.

6. In your opinion, how significant was the work of Stephen for the missionary work of the church? Explain.

CHAPTER 3

Witness in Judea and Samaria

(Acts 8:4—12:25)

"The death of Stephen," writes Rackham, "was the crucial event which started the expansion of the church" (p. 111). Apart from this event, and the general persecution which followed it, the Christian movement might have remained a small sect in Jerusalem, ignoring the missionary imperative of Acts 1:8. Now, however, the disciples are forced into the second stage of their commission: witnessing "in all Judea and Samaria." This is the theme of Acts 8:4—12:25.

The period covered, which served as a sort of transition between the strictly Jewish witness of the church (2:1—8:3) and the predominantly Gentile witness (chs. 13-28), lasted approximately nine years (A.D. 35-44). Jerusalem remained the center of Christian work, but before this section of Acts closes we see a gradual shifting of the center from Jerusalem to Antioch in Syria. Peter continues to play a prominent role, but there are also other persons to whom Luke devotes much space. Our treatment of the narrative of 8:4—12:25 will focus on (1) the witness of Philip (8:4-40), (2) the conversion of Saul (9:1-31), (3) the work of Peter (9:32—11:18), (4) the work of Barnabas (11:19-30), and (5) the persecution of Herod (12:1-25).

I. THE WITNESS OF PHILIP (8:4-40).

This is not Philip the apostle but rather the Philip who was one of the Seven (6:5). All of the apostles, we have been told (8:1), remained in Jerusalem during the period of persecution which came immediately after Stephen's death. All that we know of Philip is what may be learned from Acts 6:5; ch. 8; and 21:8, 9. From the first of these passages it is generally concluded that he was a Hellenist (see the discussion of 6:1ff.). In Acts 21:8 he is called an evangelist (i.e., one gifted to proclaim the good news). Philip is the only person in Acts so designated. Acts 21:9 informs us that he had four daughters, all of them prophetesses.

The witness of Philip, though not the exclusive concern of 8:4-40, is nonetheless the dominant theme of the passage. Luke, in narrating it, depicts three scenes in which we see Philip proclaiming Christ in Samaria (vv. 4-25), explaining the Scriptures to the Ethiopian eunuch (vv. 26-39), and preaching the Gospel from Azotus to Caesarea (v. 40).

1. *Proclaiming Christ in Samaria (vv. 4-25).* In verse 4 Luke states generally that all those who "were scattered abroad went about preaching [the Greek word is that from which we get 'evangelize'] the word." In verses 5ff. Philip is introduced as a specific example. (Later, in 11:19ff., Luke will tell of others who went beyond the borders of Palestine.)

Forced out of Jerusalem by the fury of persecution, Philip continued his work in Samaria, which lay north of Jerusalem. The Samaritans, thought of as racial and religious half-breeds by the Judeans, were descendants of the foreign settlers who replaced the Israelites deported when the northern kingdom fell. These settlers intermarried with the remaining Israelites and eventually abandoned their pagan religion to embrace a debased Judaism (cf. 2 Kings 17:24-41). Attempts were made in postexilic times to bring about reconciliation between the people of Judea and the Samaritans, but these were unsuccessful. The Samaritans' erection of a rival temple on Mt. Gerizim served to widen the cleavage between the two groups. In New Testament times Jews normally refused to associate with Samaritans (cf. John 4:9). In preaching the Gospel to the Samaritans Philip was therefore making a startling break in a deeply-ingrained racial pattern.

It is open to question whether verse 5 should be translated "the city of Samaria" (KJV, ASV), that is, the city called Samaria, or "a city of Samaria" (RSV). The Old Testament city of Samaria, capital of the district by the same name, had been rebuilt by Herod the Great and renamed Sebaste (Greek equivalent of the Latin "Augustus") in honor of the Roman emperor. Bruce thinks that if this were the city meant, Luke would more naturally have used the name Sebaste. If we follow the RSV rendering, as perhaps we should, there is no way of knowing which Samaritan city is referred to. Lake and Cadbury suggest Gitta, with which Justin Martyr connects Simon Magus (mentioned vv. 9ff.).

The substance of Philip's preaching was the messiahship of Jesus (v. 5) and the messianic kingdom (v. 12). The conversation between Jesus and the Samaritan woman (John 4) reveals that there was considerable interest among the Samaritans in the messianic hope.

Great *success* attended Philip's ministry among the Samaritans. Verses 6-8 describe the immediate results: "the crowds attended like one man to what was said by Philip" (v. 6a, Moffatt); many demonstrations of power ("signs," ASV) were witnessed (vv. 6b, 7); and there was "great rejoicing throughout that city" (v. 8, TCNT).

As a particular example of the power of Philip, the story of Simon is introduced (vv. 9-13). This man was a magician (v. 9) who by his magic acts had convinced the populace that he possessed divine powers (vv. 9-11). For "bewitched the people of Samaria" (v. 9, KJV), the NEB reads, "had swept the Samaritans off their feet." The American Bible Union Version has, "amazed the nation of Samaria."

Simon interpreted Philip's work as an undermining of his power and prestige. He therefore professed to believe. This, in light of the total context, seems to be the way we must interpret the assertion of verse 13 that "Simon also himself believed" (ASV). Another alternative is to understand the word "believed" to suggest here no more than putting credence in what Philip preached. He was convinced of the power of Jesus' name, but did not experience true saving faith.[1] He had astonished the people by trickery, but here were works for which he himself could find no explanation other than that they were genuine works of God. His main interest, it appears, was professional. "After his baptism [he] attached himself to Philip, and was in turn mystified [lit., "stood out of himself"] at seeing signs and great miracles constantly occurring" (v. 13, TCNT).

The *investigation* of Philip's work is recorded in verses 14-25. Upon hearing "that Samaria had received the word of God" (v. 14), the Jerusalem apostles sent a delegation to look into the matter. They seem to have been concerned about the genuineness of this new venture, which was "in defiance of time-honored prejudices and traditions" (Winn, p. 63). As Lampe remarks, "The preaching of the Gospel in Samaria represented a crucial moment in the first advance of Christianity" (quoted by Bruce, p. 183). Every effort had to be exerted to insure its validity. The two foremost apostles, Peter and John, were selected for the mission.

In general they found things in proper order; the Samaritan had

---

[1]Bruce concludes that the nature of Simon's belief "must remain uncertain. No doubt it was sincere as far as it went, but was very superficial and unsatisfactory. Jesus Himself," he continues, "attached little value to the faith that rested on miracles alone" (p. 179; cf. John 2:23f.).

truly believed, and Peter and John were pleased. That the apostles approved of this new direction in the work is indicated by the fact that as they returned to Jerusalem they "preached the gospel to many villages of the Samaritans" (v. 25, ASV).

One abnormal situation was discovered, however. The Holy Spirit had fallen upon none of the Samaritan believers; "they had simply been baptized into the name of the Lord Jesus" (v. 16, NIV). Peter and John therefore "prayed for them, that they might receive the Holy Spirit" (v. 15, ASV), and Luke adds that after they "placed their hands on them . . . they received the Holy Spirit" (v. 17, TCNT).

This incident has generated much theological debate. One question concerns the statement that the Spirit had not fallen upon the Samaritan believers at the time of their conversion. Some interpret this as a reference to the fullness of the Spirit, that which equips men for service (cf. H. E. Dana, *The Holy Spirit in Acts*). Others explain this as a reference not to the Spirit Himself but to supernatural gifts, that is, to manifestations of the Spirit's presence. According to this view, the apostles' prayer was that the Samaritans might have their faith confirmed by miraculous manifestations. Still others see this as a reference to the gift of the Spirit, that is, the Spirit Himself. This is the view which seems to have most to commend it.

Assuming the correctness of the third view, the question remains: Why was not the Spirit conferred upon the Samaritans at the time of their conversion? It is assumed in the New Testament that those who have truly believed have also the Spirit (cf. Rom. 5:5; 8:8-11; 1 Cor. 6:19; 12:3-13; Eph. 1:13; 4:30). In fact, this is the only instance in the entire New Testament of persons believing, being baptized, and not receiving the Holy Spirit. F. D. Bruner, who shows penetrating insight into the matter, concludes that the explanation may be found in the divine intention "to establish unequivocally for the apostles, for the despised Samaritans, and for the whole church present and future that for *God* no barriers existed for his gift of the Spirit. . . . To teach this basic and important fact . . . God withheld his gift until the apostles should see with their own eyes and . . . be instrumental with their own hands in the impartation of the gift *of God* (v. 20), merited by nothing, least of all by race or prior religion" (pp. 175, 176).

Three final observations may be made: (1) It is obvious that, though the Samaritans had not received the gift of the Spirit, they had experienced His convicting and converting influence. Otherwise they would not have truly believed. (2) The text itself gives an indication that there was something out of the ordinary about this entire situation. "Only" (v. 16b) seems to imply that the two things — baptism (confession) and reception of the Spirit — normally went together. (3) We must not try to put God in a strait jacket, but must recognize that He is sovereign in His ways of working.

Another matter in the text which has been the occasion of considerable debate is the reference to laying on of hands. Suffice it to say here that the laying on of hands was not a feature of the Pentecostal experience (2:4), nor of the filling recorded in 4:31, nor of the experience in Cornelius' house (10:44). Bruce sees no reference whatsoever to confirmation, and, following Lampe, concludes that the ritual was a token of fellowship and solidarity. (See the discussion of 6:6.)

"Now when Simon saw that through the laying on of the apostles' hands the Holy Spirit was given, he offered them money and asked them to confer on him the same power" (vv. 18, 19). This is further evidence that Simon's entire interest in Christianity was professional; he was a magician, and here was the greatest power he had ever witnessed.

For supposing that God's gift could be purchased, Peter dealt with Simon sternly. The very suggestion of such a thing was clear evidence that the man had no understanding of the essential nature of the Gospel or of the working of God's Spirit. Verses 21-23 show that Simon's "belief" (v. 13) was not true and saving faith. The fact that Luke says nothing about the subsequent life of Simon may be an indication that Peter's rebuke, though filling the man with terror, did not alter the course of his life.

Verse 25 tells of the return of Peter and John to Jerusalem, their mission accomplished. Bruce feels that the wording of the next verse implies that Philip accompanied them; it seems a logical deduction, but we cannot be sure.

2. *Explaining the Scriptures to the Ethiopian (vv. 26-39).* Sometime after the return of the preachers to Jerusalem "an angel of the Lord" (cf. 5:19) spoke to Philip (either by vision or by inward suggestion) directing him to proceed south to the road which runs from Jerusalem to Gaza. The latter was a Phoenician city, about sixty miles southwest of Jerusalem. In earlier times it had been an important junction of trade routes, and was the seat of the worship of Dagon, whose temple Samson overthrew (Judg. 16:23-31). It was prominent in the wars of the Maccabees, and was on various occasions captured or devastated by Syrians, Romans, etc. The older city was destroyed by Alexander Jannaeus in 98 B.C. "and was

known as Old Gaza after a new city of Gaza was built nearer the sea by Gabinius in 57 B.C." (Bruce, p. 186).

There were two or more roads "from Jerusalem to Gaza" (v. 26), and we are not sure which one was taken by Philip. Some think it was that which passed through Eleutheropolis. Lindsay prefers the road that went by way of Hebron through the desert hills of southern Judea.

The "man of Ethiopia" (v. 27) was treasurer under Candace, queen of the Ethiopians. Ethiopia, whose two main cities were Meroe and Napata, was in biblical times a rather vague term for the area south of Egypt. It corresponded to modern Nubia, not modern Abyssinia. Bruce explains that the king was thought to be "too sacred a personage to discharge the secular functions of royalty; these were performed on his behalf by the queen-mother, who regularly bore the dynastic title Candace" (p. 186).

That the eunuch had been to Jerusalem to "worship" suggests that he was either a proselyte to the Jewish religion or at least a God-fearing Gentile. It is thought by some that a eunuch could not have been accorded full proselyte status (cf. Deut. 23:1). At any rate, he was now "an inquirer, anxious, bewildered, but teachable" (Lindsay, I, 102), whose heart God had prepared for this moment.

Philip, following the instructions of the Spirit, ran to the eunuch's chariot and arrived just at the time when the eunuch was reading from Isaiah 53, the part which we call verse 7. (The ancients customarily read aloud even when there were no listeners.) Philip kept close to the chariot and, with some abruptness, inquired whether the man understood what he was reading. The eunuch, interpreting this as a kindly gesture, confessed his need of a guide and earnestly invited Philip to climb into the carriage and sit with him (vv. 29-33).

The eunuch courteously inquired whether the prophet who wrote the words they were reading spoke of himself or of someone else. Then Philip, taking the Isaiah passage as his text, preached to him the good news about Jesus (vv. 34, 35). The eunuch took it all in, and then, when they came to some water, he pointed it out to Philip and inquired whether there was anything to prevent him from being baptized. Verse 37 (KJV), which gives Philip's reply and the eunuch's confession, has meager textual support and is accordingly omitted by nearly all modern translations. It is not unreasonable to suppose that some such exchange as is stated in verse 37 took place, but the words are unnecessary. Doubtless Philip was convinced by the attitude and spirit of the eunuch that

Christ had entered his heart; the act of baptism, however, was itself his confession. Baptism by immersion is clearly suggested by the language of verses 38 and 39. The chariot stood still; "they both went down into the water, both Philip and the eunuch; and he baptized him. And . . . they came up out of the water . . ." (ASV).

Immediately after the baptism, Philip was "caught away" (Montgomery, "snatched away") by the Spirit. Lindsay thinks "there is no need to suppose any supernatural disappearance; Philip was compelled to depart by the same irresistible spiritual impulse that had sent him there" (I, 103). The eunuch saw Philip no more, and we hear no more of the eunuch. Irenaeus says he became a missionary to his people. At any rate, he "went on his way rejoicing" (v. 39).

Perhaps the most important lesson to be learned from this episode is what it teaches concerning the universality of the Gospel. Stifler asks: "Must not Philip reflect, when his ministry with this African was at an end, that not only were the Samaritans to hear the gospel and believe, but the ends of the earth also? . . . The distant country and the rank of Philip's hearer are certain. He was a representative of a far-off land, whom God had chosen to hear the gospel message, and Philip could not fail to get the lesson. The gospel was intended for all the world" (pp. 71, 72). Other lessons which stand out prominently are the fact of divine leadership (cf. vv. 26, 29, 39), the worth of an individual, and the theme of true witnessing (v. 35).

3. *Preaching the gospel from Azotus to Caesarea (8:40).* Philip next appeared at Azotus (the Philistine city of Ashdod), which was about twenty miles north of Gaza; the verse implies, however, that he did not remain there. "From thence he set out on a missionary journey through all the cities, ending up in Caesarea" (v. 4b, Rieu). Joppa, Lydda, and numerous other towns of the plain of Sharon lay in his path (cf. 9:32ff.). Caesarea, the site of which is about twenty-two miles south of modern Haifa, was a seaport town built by Herod the Great on the coast of Samaria.

Nothing more is told us about Philip's work, but in the one remaining reference to him in Acts (21:8, 9) he is still in Caesarea.

II. THE CALL OF SAUL OF TARSUS (9:1-31).

In his *Turning Points in History,* the late Earl of Birkenhead wrote: "of all men who may claim to have changed the course of the world's history, St. Paul must surely take first place. He altered the basic ideas of Western civilization; the whole of our history bears the marks of that busy career of impassioned teaching which the Jewish tent-maker undertook after his conversion to faith in Jesus Christ" (quoted by Scroggie, p. 252).

Our knowledge of Paul is derived almost entirely from the New Testament, the primary sources being the Book of Acts and Paul's own epistles. Only one other book in the New Testament mentions him (2 Peter 3:15), and the reference there is only an incidental one. It is generally agreed that what is said about Paul in extra-canonical literature is legendary. There is, however, a description of him given in a second-century writing *(The Acts of Paul and Thecla)* which may be authentic. There the apostle is described as "a man little of stature, thin-haired upon the head, crooked in the legs, of good state of body, with eyebrows joining, and nose somewhat hooked, full of grace: for sometimes he appeared like a man, and sometimes he had the face of an angel."

Luke has previously introduced us to Saul, making three brief but pointed references to him in connection with the story of Stephen's martyrdom (see 7:58; 8:1, 3). There we are told that he was "a young man," that he approved of the death of Stephen, and that immediately after Stephen's death he embarked on a vicious campaign to devastate the church. His fury was at fever pitch, for entering house after house he arrested both men and women, dragging them off to prison. Luke is now ready to give the center stage to Saul, and in the passage we are approaching he tells of his apprehension — his being laid hold of — by Jesus Christ (cf. Phil. 3:12). The fierce persecutor is about to become the foremost preacher of the Christian faith.[2]

The passage falls into four sections: verses 1-9, the conversion of Saul; verses 10-19a, his baptism and commission; verses 19b-22, his first preaching; and verses 23-31, early conspiracies against his life.

1. *The Conversion of Saul (9:1-9).* Few Christian people would disagree with Graham Scroggie's assertion that "of all the remarkable events in the history of the soul, probably the most remarkable is the conversion of Saul of Tarsus" (p. 251). There are three accounts of the event in the Book of Acts, one given by Luke (9:1-9) and two by Paul himself (22:6-16; 26:12-18). This fact alone is a measure of the *importance* which Luke attached to it, and the passing of the centuries has shown him to be correct in his appraisal. Saul's conversion was indeed a happening of supreme importance for the man, the church, and the world.

About the *time* of the event, there is not complete agreement,

[2]Lake and Cadbury look upon 9:1ff. as a direct continuation of 8:3, "the intervening verses being clearly a parenthesis" (p. 99).

though most interpreters place it in the mid-thirties (between A.D. 34 and 37). Earlier writers preferred 36 (Hackett, Conybeare and Howson) or 37 (Farrar, Alford). More recent scholars opt for an earlier date: Ellis suggests 33; Haenchen and Guthrie, 35. Ogg *(New Bible Dictionary,* p. 225) thinks 34 or 35 is more likely than 36 or 37. Kummel puts it as early as 31-32.

The text relates first *the circumstances* of Saul's conversion (vv. 1-3a). It occurred, we are told, at a time when he was fiercely determined to destroy Christianity. In Luke's descriptive words, he was "breathing threatening and slaughter against the disciples[3] of the Lord" (v. 1a, ASV). The TCNT, construing "threats and slaughter" as a hendiadys, renders the phrase "murderous threats." Weymouth takes the whole statement to mean that Saul's "every breath was a threat of destruction." Next, we are told that it occurred while he was in route to Damascus on a mission of persecution. Having requested and received of the high priest "letters to the Jewish congregations at Damascus" (v. 1b, 2a, TCNT), his intention was to ferret out any "who belonged to the Way,[4] whether men or women," and "take them as prisoners to Jerusalem" (v. 2b, NIV). The "letters" from the high priest, whose decrees (as president of the Sanhedrin) were binding not only for the Jews within Palestine but also (in religious matters) for those outside Palestine, were Saul's commission to demand extradition of Christians who had escaped the raging persecution in Jerusalem to build a new life in Damascus. The high priest probably was either Caiaphas or Theophilus (a son of Annas). The decision depends upon the date one assigns to this experience. Damascus, perhaps the most ancient continuously inhabited city in the world, lay on the trade route connecting Mesopotamia and Egypt. It is approximately 150 miles northeast of Jerusalem, a journey which in New Testament times required about one week of travel. In Old Testament times Damascus was the capital of Syria. There was a large Jewish community there in Paul's day. Finally, we are told that Saul's momentous experience occurred "as he neared Damascus" (v. 3a, NIV).[5] Stalker points up the drama of the occasion: "The news of Saul's coming had arrived at Damascus before him; and the little flock of Christ was praying that, if it were possible, the progress of the wolf, who was on his way to spoil the fold, might be arrested.

---

[3]The reader should watch for the various terms and titles used for Christians in this chapter.

[4]What is now called Christianity was then called "the Way" (cf. 19:9, 23; 22:4; 24:14, 22; cf. also 16:17; 18:25f.).

[5]Paul adds another detail in his account of this experience: it took place "at midday" (22:6; 26:13).

Nearer and nearer, however, he drew; he had reached the last stage of his journey; and at the sight of the place which contained his victims his appetite grew keener for the prey. But the Good Shepherd had heard the cries of his trembling flock and went forth to face the wolf on their behalf" (pp. 37, 38).

The divine encounter is described briefly but vividly in verses 3b-6. "Suddenly a light from the heavens flashed around him" (v. 3b, TCNT). The verb ("flashed"), which occurs in only one other passage in the New Testament (Acts 22:6) and not at all in classical Greek, suggests a flashing like lightning. In its uncompounded form it is found in Luke 17:24 and 24:4. Paul, in 26:13, says the light was "above the brightness of the sun" and that it shone not only around him but around his companions as well.

As he lay upon the ground to which he had fallen, he heard a voice: "Saul, Saul, why persecutest thou me?" (v. 4). In 26:14 Paul explains that the words were spoken "in the Hebrew [Aramaic] language." They imply the intimate union of Christ with His people, a concept which holds large place in the subsequent writings of Paul. Augustine, commenting on the Lord's words to the stricken Saul, said: "It was the Head in heaven crying out on behalf of the members who were still on earth."

Not knowing the identity of the speaker, Saul asked, "Who art thou, Lord?"[6] The reply answers his question ("I am Jesus whom thou persecutest," v. 5, ASV) and instructs him to "rise and enter into the city, and it shall be told thee what thou must do" (v. 6, ASV).[7] In light of Paul's later accounts of this experience (Acts 22 and 26) what he was to "do" had reference not to forgiveness but to future service. "His surrender and change of attitude seem to have been complete here on the road. But his sense of adjustment and peace in his new attitude came more slowly" (Carver, p. 93).

The "men that journeyed with" Saul (perhaps officers of justice attending him, or possibly people in a caravan with which he may have been traveling) "stood speechless" (v. 7a). Weymouth's rendering says they "were standing dumb with amazement." Luke's statement that they heard the voice (v. 7b) has been thought by some to contradict Paul's account in 22:9, where he declares that his companions "heard not the voice of him that spake to me." The

---

[6]This rendering is to be preferred over that of Goodspeed and others who translate the Greek *kurie* "sir." This is often a legitimate equivalent of the word, but in this context it seems appropriate to retain the word "Lord." Carver calls its use here "an impulsive recognition of the glorified Christ" (p. 92).
[7]The best Greek text has no equivalent for verses 5b, 6a of KJV. The essence of 5b is, however, found in 26:14 and the thought of 6a is stated in 22:10.

discrepancy is only an apparent one. It usually is explained by pointing out that the Greek case constructions of the noun ("voice") in the two passages are different. The account in chapter 9 suggests hearing the *sound* of the voice (cf. TCNT); in chapter 22 the statement is that they did not *understand* the words, that is, could not distinguish an articulate voice.[8]

At last Paul arose from the ground and, though his eyes were now open, he could see nothing. Those who were with him therefore had to take him by the hand and lead him into Damascus, where for three days he remained without sight and neither ate nor drank (vv. 8, 9). Lindsay remarks that during those three days of blindness Paul's "whole past life faded behind him" (p. 106).

2. *Saul's commission and baptism (9:10-19a).* "Ananias," described simply as "a certain disciple at Damascus" (v. 10), was God's messenger sent to baptize Saul and give him his first Christian counsel. He was a Jewish believer, respected in Damascus by both believing and unbelieving Jews (cf. 22:12, the only other biblical reference to Ananias). He may have been one of the refugees who had fled from Jerusalem after the death of Stephen; Bruce, however, doubts this, preferring to think the Gospel had at that time already made its way independently to Damascus "possibly from its northern base in Galilee" (p. 199).

It was in a vision (Phillips: "a dream") that the Lord said to him, "Arise, and go to the street which is called Straight, and inquire in the house of Judas for one named Saul, a man of Tarsus: for behold, he prayeth; and he hath seen a man named Ananias coming in, and laying his hands on him, that he might receive his sight" (vv. 11, 12, ASV). "Straight Street," on which the traditional house of Judas is pointed out to tourists, may still be seen in Damascus. Nothing is known about "Judas"; it was a common Jewish name. "He prayeth" might be rendered "he is praying." Weymouth: "for he is even now praying." That Saul had seen (obviously "in a vision," though the words are not in the best Greek text) a man named Ananias coming to him is an indication that God continued to deal with him following the experience on the road.

Ananias' hesitation is understandable: "Lord," he said, "I have heard from many of this man, how much evil he did to thy saints[9] at Jerusalem: and here he hath authority from the chief priests to bind all that call upon thy name" (vv. 13, 14, ASV). Stifler remarks

---

[8]See Bruce, p. 197, for another explanation.
[9]The first occurrence of this word in Acts as a name for Christians. Its literal meaning is "holy ones," that is, persons separated, consecrated to God.

that "the hesitation of Ananias shows how unexpected the conversion of Saul was, and how marvelous" (p. 75). The words of Ananias imply two things of historical interest: (1) that he probably had not been among those persecuted believers who had fled from Jerusalem sometime earlier (note, "I have heard") and (2) that he had had recent communication with Jerusalem (note, "here he hath authority, etc.").

God overruled Ananias' objections, explaining that Saul was "a chosen vessel . . . to bear my name before the Gentiles and kings, and the children of Israel" (v. 15, ASV). In adding "for I will show him how many things he must suffer for my name's sake" (v. 16, ASV), God was in effect telling Ananias to think no more about how much suffering Saul had caused. The meaning of "the Gentiles" should not go unnoticed. "The work so long delayed among the Jews is now to extend to the nations, for the man is selected and designated to effect it" (Stifler, p. 75). The Greek word for "show" means simply to point out, though there may be in it a connotation of warning.

Ananias required no further prompting. Convinced of God's will in the matter, he went directly to Judas' house. Having entered, he laid his hands on Saul and said, "Brother Saul, the Lord, even Jesus, who appeared unto thee in the way which thou camest, hath sent me, that thou mayest receive thy sight, and be filled with the Holy Spirit" (v. 17, ASV). Note the following: (1) The address ("Brother Saul") is strikingly tender and must have cheered the heart of the former persecutor. (2) The laying on of hands in this instance was not a rite performed by an apostle, but by a man of whom nothing is said about official rank. (On the laying on of hands, see the discussion of 6:5). Perhaps we are to see in it the suggestion that Saul's ministry was to be totally independent of the Twelve, his fellow apostles. (3) The laying on of hands was a part of Christ's commissioning of Saul. In this act Ananias, though not called an apostle, was himself "a duly commissioned apostle. But he was more; he was a duly authorized prophet. It was as the spokesman of Christ — as His very mouthpiece — that he went to Saul . . . Ananias uttered the words, but as he did so it was Christ himself who commissioned Saul to be his Ambassador" (Bruce, pp. 200, 201). (4) The filling with the Spirit was the necessary equipment for carrying out Saul's commission.

3. *Saul's first preaching (9:19b-22).* Saul, unlike any of the new converts mentioned earlier in the record, begins immediately to preach. The substance of his preaching was "Jesus." Doubtless he proclaimed that he was truly alive (not dead, as he had thought

earlier). Moreover, he asserted that "he is the Son of God" (not an impostor) and convincingly proved to his audiences that "Jesus is the Christ" (RSV). The Greek word behind "proving" (v. 22) suggests the putting of the prophetic Scriptures alongside their fulfillment, "in order to prove that Jesus was the Messiah of whom they spoke" (Bruce, pp. 203, 204).

Such preaching (and by such a preacher) created a sensation in Damascus. All who heard him "continued to be amazed [Phillips: "were staggered"], and were saying, 'Is this not he who in Jerusalem destroyed those who called on this name, and who had come here for the purpose of bringing them bound before the chief priests?' " (v. 21, NASB).

The visit of Paul to Arabia (cf. Gal. 1:15-18) occurred in the period of time which elapsed between the narrative of verse 22 and the incident recorded in verses 23ff. Luke does not record the event, but he does leave room for it (note v. 23, "when many days were fulfilled").

4. *Early conspiracies against Saul's life (vv. 23-31).* Two conspiracies against Paul's life are recorded in verses 23-31. The first occurred in Damascus, to which he returned when he left Arabia. (We learn from Gal. 1:15-18 that the "many days" of verse 23 amounted to about three years.) Paul tells of this experience in 2 Corinthians 11:32, 33.

The second conspiracy, which occurred in Jerusalem, is recorded in verses 26-31. Observe the following in studying this paragraph: (1) This was Saul's first visit to Jerusalem following his conversion. From Galatians 1:15-18, we learn that he had been a Christian about three years at the time. Carver calls attention to the contrast in Saul's "actual return to Jerusalem with that of his purpose three years before. Truly he has learned something of the power of Jesus in this time" (p. 99). (2) The visit recorded here is the one mentioned in Galatians 1:18-20. (3) The disciples, not having had contact with him since his departure from Jerusalem on a mission of persecution, were fearful of receiving Saul into their fellowship (v. 26). It was Barnabas (cf. 4:35, 36) who befriended him and convinced the apostles that Saul had been truly converted (v. 27). Saul thus is "the first man of whom we read whose application to join the Jerusalem church was rejected" (Carver, p. 99). (4) Saul's preaching in Jerusalem was especially directed to "the Grecian Jews" (cf. 6:1, 9), the group to whom he, a non-Palestinian, may have been best known, and the group which had initiated the action which resulted in Stephen's martyrdom. Their reaction to Saul was no different: "they were seeking to kill him"

(v. 29). (5) In 22:17-21 Paul informs us that the Lord appeared to him at this time in a vision in the Temple and commanded him to leave Jerusalem. Paul protested the role he played in the death of Stephen, implying that he was willing to suffer the same fate that befell Stephen. The Lord, however, had other work for Saul. (6) Saul, with the aid of the brethren, left Jerusalem and went by way of Caesarea to Tarsus, his birthplace. He was still here some time later when Barnabas found him and took him to Antioch (11:25, 26).

Verse 31 is a sort of footnote (actually one of the summaries typical of Acts) to the account of Saul's conversion. "So," the first word of the verse, suggests that the peace and growth of the church were in some sense consequences of Saul's dramatic conversion.

The conversion of Saul was of utmost importance for all of his subsequent thought and action. It was in this experience that he learned the truth about Jesus (Messiah, Son of God, Lord of glory), the depth of divine grace and mercy (1 Cor. 15:10; 1 Tim. 1:12-14), the meaning of faith-righteousness (Phil. 3:4ff.), the concept of the believer's union with Christ (cf. 9:4, 5). Indeed, Paul's "whole theology is nothing but the explication of his own conversion" (Stalker, p. 40).

In addition, Saul's conversion is one of the strongest proofs of the truth of Christianity. Two hundred years ago two Englishmen (Gilbert West and George Lyttleton) decided to make a major attack on the Christian religion. Mr. West was to show that the resurrection of Christ had never occurred, and Lord Lyttleton was to prove that the account of Saul's conversion was not factual. Some time later, the two men came together to compare notes and each admitted he had been convinced of the truth of the subject he set out to attack and of the truth of the Christian religion. Lyttleton later wrote that "the conversion and apostleship of St. Paul, duly considered, was of itself a demonstration sufficient to prove Christianity to be a divine revelation" *(Observations on the Conversion of St. Paul).*

III. THE JOURNEYS OF PETER (9:32—11:18).

Peter, of course, has figured prominently in the narrative which precedes this section. In Acts 1:13 his name appears in the list of apostles who returned to Jerusalem following Christ's ascension. He was apparently moderator of the assembly which selected a replacement for Judas in the apostolate (1:15ff.). It was he who was principal preacher on the Day of Pentecost (2:14ff.); and he, along with John, was the key figure in the healing of the lame man at the Beautiful Gate — an incident which precipitated the first wave of opposition to the Christian movement (chs. 3, 4). His role in the narrative of chapter 5 is equally prominent: the Ananias and Sapphira episode (5:1-11), the burst of miraculous demonstrations which followed (5:12-16), and the arrest and imprisonment of the apostles which culminated in their being threatened and beaten by the Sanhedrin (5:17-42). A glimpse of Peter's earlier missionary work is provided in Acts 8:14-25.

It appears that until the incidents recorded in the present passage Peter made his headquarters in Jerusalem. True, there had been a brief mission to Samaria (8:14-25), but he returned to Jerusalem and was still in Jerusalem when Saul returned to the city (Gal. 1:18). At this point, however, he enters upon an itinerant ministry which takes him to various parts of Judea and Samaria. Perhaps the freedom from persecution and the period of new growth (9:31) provided the incentive. The story focuses on four places: Lydda (9:32-35), Joppa (9:36—10:23a), Caesarea (10:23b-48), and Jerusalem (11:1-18).

1. *Peter at Lydda (9:31-35)*. Peter's departure from Jerusalem probably occurred shortly after Paul had left the city (9:30), though Lake and Cadbury think it may be the continuation of 8:25, where Peter is last mentioned (p. 107). Haenchen thinks Peter's intention was to make "a kind of tour of inspection" (p. 338). Chrysostom comments that like the commander of an army Peter "went about inspecting the ranks, what part was compact, what in good order, what needed his presence" (quoted by Lindsay, p. 111). Zahn, using a different figure, says that "Peter . . . came . . . in fulfillment . . . of the injunction to feed the flock, the young sheep as well as the old" (quoted by Haenchen, p. 338).

In the course of his travels "throughout all parts" (v. 32, ASV) of the country[10] Peter came eventually to visit "the saints that dwelt at Lydda" (v. 32). This is modern Lod (or Ludd), located in the Plain of Sharon twenty-three miles northwest of Jerusalem. In Old Testament times it was called Lod (cf. 1 Chron. 8:12; Neh. 11:35), and in the early centuries of the Christian era it was known as Diospolis. After the destruction of Jerusalem, it was a famous center for rabbinical learning. The "saints" who dwelt there at the time of Peter's visit may have been refugees from Jerusalem who

---

[10]The Greek reads simply "through all," leaving the noun to be supplied. The ASV has "throughout all parts"; KJV, "throughout all quarters"; Weymouth, "to town after town"; NIV, "as Peter traveled about the country." Hackett renders it "through all the believers in that part of the country" (p. 126).

fled that city after the death of Stephen. Another possibility is that they were converts of Philip (cf. 8:40).

Here Peter found "a certain man named Aeneas" (v. 33). The name suggests that he was a Hellenist, and the context implies he was a Christian. This latter is not expressly stated, however, and Lake and Cadbury think that he was not a believer. Aeneas had been bed-ridden with paralysis for eight years (v. 33).[11] Matthew Henry adds: "Christ chose such patients as those whose diseases were incurable in course of nature, to show how desperate the case of fallen mankind was when He undertook their cure."

The verb in Peter's statement, "Jesus Christ healeth thee" (v. 34, ASV), employs what grammarians call the aoristic present. The force of it is: "this instant Jesus Christ is healing you" (cf. Haenchen, p. 338). In response to Peter's command to get up and make his bed,[12] Aeneas rose to his feet at once (v. 34b). With a degree of exaggeration it is added that "all that dwelt at Lydda and in [the Plain of] Sharon [a beautiful and fertile district, extending from Joppa to Caesarea] saw him, and they turned to the Lord" (v. 35, ASV). The impression is of a great revival. In view of the subsequent account of Cornelius' conversion, we should understand the "all" of the present verse to refer to Jews. Haenchen thinks the word "God" rather than "Lord" probably would have been used had the reference been to the turning of Gentiles.

2. *Peter at Joppa (9:36—10:23a).* Joppa, modern Jaffa (or Yafo), is on the Mediterranean coast thirty-five miles northwest of Jerusalem and about twelve miles northwest of Lydda. The modern community is actually a suburb of Tel Aviv (which is sometimes designated Tel Aviv-Jaffa). The ancient city, mentioned in the Old Testament several times (cf. 2 Chron. 2:16; Jonah 1:3) and referred to also in Egyptian records dating from the fifteenth century B.C., served as a seaport for Jerusalem. In Joshua 19:46 it is called Japho.

At Joppa two notable events occurred: the raising of Dorcas to life (9:36-43) and Peter's preparation for witnessing to the Gentiles (10:1-23a). The circumstances surrounding the first of these was the occasion for Peter's removal from Lydda to Joppa.

(1) *The restoration of Dorcas to life (9:36-43).* This is the first instance recorded in Acts of a person being raised from the dead.

----

[11]The Greek construction could be rendered "since he was eight years old" (cf. Lake and Cadbury), but this is not a widely accepted translation.
[12]The Greek might be more literally translated: "spread thy bed for thyself," the reflexive pronoun alluding to the fact that others had done this for Aeneas for years.

Dorcas is only the second woman mentioned by name in Acts since the account of Pentecost (ch. 2), the other being Sapphira (ch. 5). Nothing is known of Dorcas except what is told here, but she is introduced with some fullness of detail. That she was a Christian is evident from the reference to her as "a certain disciple" (v. 36). Her name in Aramaic was "Tabitha" (v. 36), and from this we may conclude that she was a Jewish Christian. Her Aramaic name, meaning "gazelle," was translated into Greek as "Dorcas," which means the same thing. Her generosity is reflected in the statement that she "was full of good works and almsdeeds" (v. 36, ASV). "Which she did" (v. 36) translates an imperfect tense, suggesting that good works and almsdeeds were habitually done by her. Weymouth: "Her life was full of the good and charitable actions which she was constantly doing." Verse 39 points up that these had especially endeared her to her friends. That her husband is not mentioned suggests that she had never married or, as is more likely, was a widow.

Following her death, which seems to have occurred after only a short illness, her body was duly prepared but was not buried at once. Instead they laid the body "in a room upstairs" (v. 37, Weymouth). Lindsay remarks that "there was faith in the act" (I, 112). The disciples at Joppa, upon hearing that Peter was in Lydda (only twelve miles away, three hours on foot), sent two men to him entreating him to come to their aid. That they should come with such a request after Dorcas had already died is somewhat remarkable. They must have felt that Peter could restore her to life. Their words, "Delay not to come on unto us" (v. 38c), were simply a polite way of saying, "Please come to us" (Bruce, p. 212).

Peter got up at once and went with them. When he arrived at the house, he was taken immediately to the upper chamber, where Dorcas' body lay. "The widows" who "stood by him weeping" (v. 39) are thought by some to have been "an organization for Christian charity like that presided over by the Seven in Jerusalem" (Lindsay, I, 113). Those who interpret in this manner point out that Philip, one of the Seven, had probably preached in Joppa, which was near Azotus (8:40). It is more likely that these were widows who had benefited from the charitable deeds of Dorcas. As they stood around Peter in tears, they showed him "the coats and garments which Dorcas made, while she was with them" (v. 39, ASV). The thought probably is that they were wearing the clothes which Dorcas had given them.

Peter's actions in the upper chamber are reminiscent of the actions of Jesus in the house of Jairus. All the mourners, who were in this instance real (not hired), were sent out of the room; the apostle "kneeled down, and prayed" (v. 40). Lechler comments: "This prayer is the essential feature by which the resurrection of Tabitha is distinguished from that of the daughter of Jairus. Jesus, without any preceding prayer, took the dead child by the hand, and recalled her to life; but Peter does not do so until he has prayed to the Lord for the miracle" (quoted by Lindsay, p. 113). After he had prayed, Peter turned to the body and commanded, "Tabitha, arise"[13] (v. 40). Then she opened her eyes and, seeing Peter, sat up. Whereupon the apostle gave her his hand, raised her up from the pallet on which she had been laid, and gave her back alive to "the saints and widows" (v. 41). The latter group may be mentioned separately, not because they were entirely distinct from the "saints" (i.e., Christians) but perhaps because not *all* of them were saints. "No doubt," says Bruce, "Dorcas' charity extended beyond the bounds of the local Christian group" (p. 212).

This miracle, like the one at Lydda, resulted in spiritual revival. It "became known throughout all Joppa: and many believed on the Lord" (v. 42, ASV).

Verse 43, which is the connecting link with the next narrative, informs us that Peter did not return to Lydda but "abode many days in Joppa with one Simon a tanner" (ASV). Lindsay thinks the "many days" may refer to a period of more than a year (p. 113). That the apostle was residing with a tanner is also significant. The tanner's trade was considered unclean by the Jews; in fact, a woman whose husband became a tanner was thought to have grounds for divorce. "Peter's lodging with such a man," writes Bruce, "was a mark of his increasing emancipation from cere-monial traditions" (p. 213). "Peter," comments Lindsay, "had got half-way to Cornelius and the Gentiles when he lodged with a tanner. . . . God's providence leads men step by step" (I, 113).

Haenchen thinks the two accounts which close chapter 9 (Peter's experiences at Lydda and Joppa) reveal that Luke has ordered his material with "thorough deliberation." The history of the advance of the Gospel has been narrated in a manner which shows that "the whole of the country west of the Jordan, from Ashdod north-ward almost as far as Caesarea, has now become Christian. Congre-gations have been established in Judea, Samaria and Galilee (there are no reports about the country east of Jordan). The task in Palestine proper has been accomplished, and it is time for the Christian mission to seek goals farther afield" (p. 341, 342).

---

[13]The Aramaic of Peter's words is identical with the words of Jesus to the daughter of Jairus, except for one letter (Ta*b*itha instead of Ta*l*itha).

(2) *The preparation for witnessing to the Gentiles* (10:1-23a). The Cornelius episode, which occupies a central place in the plan of Acts, is of singular importance because it was the first instance of the admission of a Gentile into the church in total disregard of Old Testament legislation. That Luke considered it to be of far-reaching significance is indicated by the relatively large amount of space which he devotes to it — all of chapter 10 and about half of chapter 11. The significance of this event is further underscored by Luke's use of repetition. Cornelius' vision is described four times, Peter's twice; and 11:5-18 contains a summary of the entire story of chapter 10. Luke's account of the episode involves happenings in three cities: Joppa, Caesarea, and Jerusalem.

The idea which pervades the present section (10:1-23a) is preparation. Luke's intention was to show how Peter especially (and, indirectly, the whole church) was made ready for the reception of Gentiles within the gospel fold. Cornelius and Peter were instructed about the same time, each by an appropriate vision.

Stifler raises several questions which the reader should consider as he approaches this portion of Acts: "Why must Jerusalem and Judea have such overwhelming proof of the Lord's purpose to save the Gentiles? Has not Samaria been gladly welcomed among the Jewish believers? Has not the Eunuch been baptized? Has not Saul been converted that he may be sent to the Gentiles?" Then he calls attention to the great gulf which separated Jews and Gentiles — "much wider and deeper than that between the Jews and the Samaritans. . . . The separation was complete. It was not a matter of a day, but of centuries. It was worse than Hindu caste. The chasm between blacks and whites in this country," he continues, "is as nothing compared with that between Jew and Greek. The touch of the latter was defiling, his food was an abomination to the devout Israelite, and his religion blasphemy" (pp. 81, 82).

There are two scenes in the narrative before us; one, almost parenthetical, is set in Caesarea and concerns Cornelius (vv. 1-8); the other is set in Joppa and centers in the experience of Peter (vv. 9-23a).

a. The vision of Cornelius (vv. 1-8). Luke's account is concise and to the point. Verses 1, 2 introduce us to Cornelius; verses 3-6 describe his vision; and verses 7, 8 record his response to the vision.

Verses 1, 2. Three matters are brought out in the description of Cornelius:[14] his home, his position, and his religious character. His

---

[14]The name was a common one. It was in fact the family name of Sulla and was taken to be the family name of thousands of slaves who had been liberated by him (Haenchen, p. 346; Lake and Cadbury, p. 112).

home was "in Caesarea," a seaport city which was approximately thirty miles north of Joppa. In an earlier time Caesarea was called Strato's Tower. Rebuilt by Herod the Great, it was in New Testament times the home of the Roman procurator (Pilate, Felix, Festus, etc.) of Judea and headquarters for his occupation army. Lindsay calls Caesarea "the great Gentile city of Palestine" and observes that in the part of Acts which treats of the transition from Jewish to Gentile Christianity, "it was natural that Caesarea and not Jerusalem should be the center of Christian activity" (I, 114). Earlier references in Acts to the city are 8:40 and 9:30.

His official position was "centurion of the band called the Italian band" (v. 1b, (ASV). A centurion was an officer in the Roman army with a company of one hundred men under his command. Bruce explains that "his responsibilities corresponded to those of a modern army captain" but that "his status was that of a non-commissioned officer." Those who held this rank, he continues, "were the backbone of the Roman army" (p. 215). Centurions are mentioned in the New Testament more than twenty times, and without exception they appear in a good light (cf. Matt. 8:5; 27:54; Acts 27:31, 43). A regular "band" ("cohort," ABUV; "regiment," TCNT; "troop," Beck) was made up of six hundred infantrymen (i.e., six "centuries"), under the command of a tribune. Haenchen speaks of this particular "band" as "a battalion of archers" and thinks it was probably an auxiliary, not a regular, unit known as the *Cohors II Miliaria Italica Civium Romanorum Voluntariorum*. This auxiliary cohort, consisting of one thousand (note "miliaria") men rather than six hundred, was probably a unit "formed originally in Italy from freedmen. . . . It was later transferred to Syria, and is known to have been there from shortly before A.D. 69 down to the second century" (p. 346).

Cornelius' *religious character* is described as follows: "a devout man, and one that feared God with all his house, who gave much alms to the people, and prayed to God always" (v. 2, ASV). "Devout" men who "feared God" were Gentiles who believed in the God of Israel and took part in synagogue services without becoming full-fledged proselytes to the Jewish religion. Sometimes they were called "proselytes of the gate." Such persons were uncircumcised and were therefore looked upon by the Jews as unclean. That Cornelius "gave such alms" to the Jewish people is indicative of his generous spirit. This is rather remarkable, when we remember that he was associated with overbearing Rome and was commander of a company of foreign soldiers ready to crush any Jewish uprising. A further index to Cornelius' character is provided by the reference to his habit of prayer. Acts 11:14 appears to suggest that he was praying for guidance about the way of salvation. He was thus "one of those Gentiles who, in an age of fading faiths, had become attached to the pure monotheism of the Jews" (Lindsay, I, 114).

Verses 3-6 describe the vision. It came at "about the ninth hour of the day" (i.e., at 3 P.M.), which was an hour of prayer and the time of the offering of the evening oblation. Haenchen thinks the mention of the time was intended to point up "the reality of the occurrence; it takes place in broad daylight" (p. 346). In the vision Cornelius "distinctly saw . . . an angel from God come . . . and call him by name (v. 3, TCNT). The Greek word for "distinctly" is rendered in the KJV by "evidently," in ASV by "openly." Its use here is another device of Luke to emphasize the reality of Cornelius' experience.

The centurion "stared at the angel in terror" (v. 4, Moffatt) and asked "What is it, Lord?" In reply the angel made a statement ("Thy prayers and thine alms are gone up for a memorial[15] before God," v. 4b, ASV), to reassure Cornelius that his prayer and almsgiving had acepted by God as a worthy oblation, issued a command (send to Joppa," etc., v. 5), and gave necessary instructions about where to find Peter (v. 6). In 11:14 it is explained that the angel added that Peter would tell Cornelius what he must do to be saved. Cornelius was earnestly seeking light, and God was about to give him more light. The reference to Peter's residing with a tanner was perhaps intended to encourage Cornelius, for he would know by this that Peter was not bound by the usual Jewish rigidity.

Verses 7 and 8 describe Cornelius' response to the vision. In short, it was immediate obedience. As soon as the angel had departed (it was now past 3 P.M.), he summoned "two of his household servants" and one of his military aides who was "a devout soldier" like himself (i.e., one who was seeking the truth about God). After telling these three men everything that had happened to him, Cornelius sent them off to Joppa. It is often remarked that God had to speak to Cornelius only once; a little later, he will have to tell Peter three times what he wants him to do.

b. The vision of Peter (vv. 9-16). The messengers from Cornelius walked through the night (pausing from time to time, of course, for rest) and approached Joppa about noon ("the sixth hour") the day following his vision. It was about this time that Peter "went up upon the housetop to pray" (v. 9, ASV). Many pious Jews made the noon hour a time of prayer although it was not one of the

---

[15]The only other instance in which the Greek word for "memorial" is used in the New Testament is by Jesus about the loving act of Mary of Bethany (Matt. 26:13; Mark 14:9).

fixed times for public prayer (cf. Ps. 55:17; Dan. 6:10). The flat roof, with its parapet (Deut. 22:8) and awning, was an inviting place for meditation and prayer.

While on the roof Peter became very hungry[16] and desired something to eat. Verse 10b suggests that he called downstairs for some food. It was while the family, or the servants, were preparing this that "he fell into a trance" (v. 10). The Greek word, of which the English "ecstasy" is a transliteration, properly denotes a "distraction" or "disturbance" of mind caused by a shock. Its literal meaning is a putting out of place, and from that comes the thought of driving out of one's senses. Sometimes the word is used to express simple astonishment. Here it denotes "a trance, an ecstasy in which a person passes out of himself" (Knowling, p. 253). While in this state Peter saw a vision (vv. 11-16), the details of which are familiar. Bruce suggests that it was "no doubt because of [Peter's] hunger that the vision centered around food" (p. 218). The "vessel" (v. 1) in which were all manner of animals was like "a great sheet" (TCNT, "something like a great sail"; NEB, "a thing . . . that looked like a great sheet of sail-cloth").

The dialogue between Peter and the "voice" that came to him is made more impressive by being spoken three times (vv. 13-16a). Immediately after the third exchange the vessel was taken up into heaven — "drawn up out of sight" (Weymouth).

c. The visit of the messengers (vv. 17-23a). When the messengers arrived at Simon the tanner's house, Peter was still on the roof, wondering what the meaning of his vision might be. "Much perplexed" (v. 17, ASV) suggests that he was completely at a loss to explain it. Peter was conscious of having been taught a lesson, but what the lesson was he did not know: "Was it that henceforth he should eat what he had before thought unclean, or had it wider application?" (Lindsay, I, 116).

Haenchen, observing that a tanner would not possess an imposing house separated from the street by a courtyard, translates verse 18: "They came to the door and asked, shouting aloud: Is Simon, also called Peter, lodging here?"

The Spirit advises Peter that three men are seeking him (v. 19) and commands him to go downstairs and accompany the men without any misgivings. The Spirit encouraged Peter by explaining that it was He who had sent them (v. 20). Obediently, the apostle went down (perhaps by an outside stairway), introduced himself,

---

[16]The word for "hungry" (v. 10, ASV) is a compound form found only here in the New Testament. The prepositional prefix gives it intensive force.

and inquired of the messengers the purpose of their visit (v. 21). They, in turn, gave a brief account of Cornelius' experience, emphasizing his religious character and reputation, and that it was a holy angel who instructed him to contact Peter (v. 22). By this time the meal which Peter had requested was probably ready. The messengers doubtless shared it with him; then, because they had traveled a long way and were weary, they were invited to lodge the rest of the day and all night in Simon's house (v. 23a). It is worthy of note that Peter at this point does not recoil from entertaining Gentiles. The essential meaning of his vision, no doubt made clear by the explanation of Cornelius' messengers, is now understood by him: "No limits of race, or position in society, no barriers of circumstances or upbringing, can separate men from each other" (Lindsay, I, 116).

3. *Peter at Caesarea (10:23b-48).* On the day after Peter's rooftop vision he set out (Moffatt: "he was up and off," v. 23b) with the three messengers for Caesarea, taking along six (cf. 11:12) members of the congregation in Joppa. The latter action indicates that Peter was expecting something momentous to occur, and he desired to have witnesses to the event. Carver, observing that Peter was embarking on "an heretical errand," calls his decision to have the six brethren accompany him " 'long-headed' foresight" (p. 110).

(1) *The meeting of Peter and Cornelius* (vv. 24-33). On the day following — the third day after Cornelius' vision, the second day after Peter's experience — they reached Caesarea (v. 24a). The centurion was eagerly awaiting their arrival, having called together (cf. 11:14) "his kinsmen and close friends" (v. 24b, RSV). The account points up the complete faith which Cornelius had in the revelations made to him in his vision.

When Peter entered "the house" (v. 25a, Weymouth, Moffatt, NIV; TCNT reads "the city" instead of "the house"; Haenchen understands "the gateway"), Cornelius met him, and falling down at his feet, "worshipped him" (v. 25b). The Greek word for "worshipped," which means "to go down to the knees to," "to do obeisance to," denotes an act of reverence accorded either to man or to God. Since the centurion acknowledged the God of Israel as the one true God, it is doubtful that he intended this as an act of religious homage. "Paid reverence to" may therefore be a better rendering than "worshipped." The TCNT has "bowed to the ground"; Rotherham, "did homage"; Goodspeed, "made obeisance to"; NEB, "bowed to the ground in deep reverence." Lindsay writes: "Cornelius was a Roman, and a soldier, and was not accustomed to make Oriental salutations; if he went out to meet Peter, and made low obeisance, it was because he looked on Peter as a supernatural messenger" (p. 117) — or as Haenchen says, "a heavenly visitant" (p. 350). Peter, however, "lifted him to his feet" (v. 26a, Goodspeed), saying as he did so: "Stand up, I am only a man like yourself" (v. 26b, TCNT). Then, as they continued to talk, Peter "went into the house[17] and found a great crowd had gathered" (v. 27, Williams).

Peter reminded the assembled group that Jews considered it unlawful for a Jewish man to associate with, or even to visit, a Gentile,[18] but he went on to explain that God had revealed to him that he should call no man common or unclean (v. 28). Carver: "still in my case God showed me to call nobody common or unclean that is human" (p. 111).

Cornelius, at the request of Peter (v. 29), recounted the events which led to his sending for the apostle (vv. 30-32). Then he thanked him — this is the force of the words "thou hast done well that thou art come" (v. 33a) — for coming, and in effect invited him to begin speaking "all things that have been commanded thee of the Lord" (v. 33, ASV). "Peter has a great opportunity with this eager, reverent, expectant audience, the first company of Gentiles to hear the gospel, and by their own invitation" (Carver, p. 112).

(2) *The message of Peter* (vv. 34-43). Three general observations may be made: (a) By prefacing the sermon with the words, "And Peter opened his mouth, and said" (v. 34a, ASV), Luke stresses the solemnity of the occasion and of the address which follows (cf. Matt. 5:2; Acts 2:14; 8:35; cf. Haenchen). (b) The sermon follows the same general pattern as that of the message on the day of Pentecost (ch. 2). (c) The same pattern or outline is followed in the gospel of Mark, who, according to tradition, later became Peter's interpreter.

The message, which no doubt is given in condensed form, is simple and straightforward. It consists of the following: (a) A brief *introduction,* which takes the form of a statement concerning the character of God (vv. 34b, 35). "God is no respecter of persons," affirms Peter; in fact, "in every nation he that feareth him, and worketh righteousness, is acceptable to him" (ASV). The meaning is not that Cornelius was already saved and that in all nations men like him are saved with no knowledge of Christ; rather, the thought

---

[17]These words (though there is no equivalent in the Greek for "house") suggest that in verse 25a we should probably supply "the city" or "the gate" rather than "the house."

[18]No Old Testament passage expressly forbids such social contact, but the rabbis so interpreted the Old Testament and made the restriction a binding custom.

is that through Christ men of all nations can be saved even though they are not Jews. (b) The *theme,* which takes the form of a statement about Jesus of Nazareth (vv. 36-43). Attention is directed to His life and works (v. 38); His crucifixion and death (v. 39); His resurrection (vv. 40, 41), which was accomplished by God (v. 40) and attested by witnesses (v. 41); His appointment to be Judge (v. 42), which is by the authority of God and over all men; and His offer of forgiveness (v. 43), which is open to "every one that believeth on him."

(3) *The conversion of Cornelius and his household* (vv. 44-48). Peter did not get to finish his sermon (cf. 2:37), for while he was yet preaching "the Holy Spirit fell on all them that heard the word" (v. 44, ASV).[19] Bruce, quoting Chase, speaks of this as the "Pentecost of the Gentile world" (p. 229). The gift of the Spirit came upon the hearers in the very way in which it had come upon the earliest disciples (cf. 2:1-4), without any human intervention. God makes no distinction between Jews and Gentiles; "he has enough and to spare for all those who call upon him" (Rom. 10:12, Knox).

The descent of the Spirit upon Cornelius' household was outwardly manifested by their speaking "with tongues" and their magnifying God (v. 46; cf. 2:4, 11). Both things are reminiscent of Pentecost and served as indubitable evidence that these people — Gentiles though they were — had been truly accepted of God. Bruce adds: "Apart from such external manifestations, none of the Jewish Christians present, perhaps not even Peter himself, would have been so ready to accept the fact that the Spirit had really come upon them" (p. 230). Peter's Jewish companions, witnessing all of this, "were amazed" (v. 45, ASV). Bruner sees in their amazement evidence "that here as at Pentecost tongues came not as a sought evidence of the baptism of the Holy Spirit but as a complete surprise. . . . Speaking in tongues," he explains, "occurs in Acts 2 and 10, but in both instances the occurrence is *unsought, unexpected,* and *undemanded*" (p. 192). Elsewhere the same writer says that tongues had evidential value "not because they were expected, required, or usual, but precisely because they were unexpected, unrequired, and unusual — resembled only by Pentecost

---

[19]Luke records four occasions on which the Spirit descended: at Pentecost (on the original disciples, ch. 2), on the Samaritans (ch. 8), at Caesarea (on Cornelius and other Gentiles), and at Ephesus (on John's "disciples," ch. 19). It is worthy of note that (1) each occasion represents a different class of persons, (2) each (except for that recorded in ch. 19) represents a new advance or stage in witnessing, and (3) in each instance the experience is followed by extraordinary signs.

— convincing even the most hard-necked that God wanted the Gentiles as well as the Jews among his people. Had there been faith to believe that Jesus Christ is 'Lord of all' (10:36) there may have been no need for this drama. The clear teaching of the New Testament is that the need for the spectacular is more often a feature of unbelief than of belief, for in the words which our Lord often repeated: 'an evil and adulterous generation seeks for a sign' " (pp. 191, 192). Peter's words in 11:15-17 appear to suggest that the tongues-speaking in the house of Cornelius was the same as that of Pentecost.

Peter, being convinced that Cornelius and his household had been converted, suggested that there was no reason why baptism should be denied them (v. 47). Then he directed that they should be baptized, perhaps delegating the responsibility for administering the rite to one of his Jewish companions (v. 48).

4. *Peter at Jerusalem (11:1-18).* The admission of Gentiles into the fellowship of the Christian community was an event of such magnitude that the news of it spread quickly (v. 1). The present passage is the story of the reaction of the brethren in Judea; especially, it tells how they were led to accept the new state of affairs.

(1) *The charge against Peter* (vv. 1-3). The reader should observe the following: (a) The source of the charge: "they that were of the circumcision" (v. 2). This phrase seems to designate not all the Jewish believers but a group within the Jerusalem church especially zealous of the law. Lindsay remarks that the phrase "marks the beginning of evil and of separation in the Apostolic Church. The words had previously been used to designate all Jewish Christians, but now they seem to refer to one party among the Jewish believers, to the Judaizers who were unable to believe that Gentiles could enter the church save through Judaism" (I, 123). This faction became inveterate enemies of Paul and caused much trouble in the church (cf. Titus 1:10; Acts 15:5; the letter to the Galatians).

(b) The nature of the charge. They seem not to have objected to Peter's preaching to Gentiles; it was his fraternizing with them that distressed the circumcision party. "Thou wentest in to men uncircumcised, and didst eat with them" (v. 3; cf. Mark 2:16; Luke 15:2).

(2) *The explanation of Peter* (vv. 4-17). The apostle recounted his housetop experience, emphasizing his initial unwillingness to heed the command of God (vv. 4-10); explained that it was the Spirit who bade him go with the messengers from Cornelius, and that he was expressly charged to make "no distinction" (v. 12a,

ASV; Weymouth, "without any misgivings"); brought forward the six Jewish brethren who accompanied him, pointing out that they had seen and heard all that transpired at the house of Cornelius (vv. 12b-15; note *"we* entered . . . he told *us"*)[20]; and told of how the approval of God had been demonstrated by the gift of the Holy Spirit "on them, even as on us at the beginning" (vv. 15, 16).[21] Finally, the apostle suggested that if his actions had been otherwise he would have been standing against God: "who was I, what power had I, to stay God's hand? (v. 17, Knox; Rieu, "who was I to try to stand in God's way?"). The translations quoted show that two ideas flow into the question: (1) Who was *I,* to thwart *God?* (2) How was I in a *position* to thwart God? (cf. Haenchen, p. 355).

(3) *The verdict for Peter* (v. 18). After hearing Peter's explanation, his opponents "were silenced"; RSV [Carver, "became quiet"; *Modern Language,* "quieted down"; NIV, "had no further objections"] "but broke out into praise of God. 'So even to the Gentiles,' they exclaimed, 'God has granted the repentance which leads to Life!' " (TCNT). Lindsay thinks the Greek tenses in the first half of the verse (three aorists and a present participle) "make the scene more vivid — a breathless pause, and then a continuous utterance of praise" (I, 125).

Carver sees the use of an aorist verb ("granted") rather than a perfect in the last half of the verse as having special significance. "The perfect," he explains, "would concede an established principle; the aorist . . . concedes the one incident but does not commit them to the principle for permanent application. They allow it now, but will oppose it later, conditionally at least" (p. 121).

The following teachings may be derived from the Cornelius episode: First, we learn here that the Gospel is intended for all people. It follows then, that if God wants all people to hear, it is our duty to get it to them. Second, we learn that Christian fellowship transcends all racial, social, and cultural differences. Those whom God receives we should receive. Third, we learn that the careful observance of religious duties is not enough to save one. Cornelius, who prayed to God regularly and gave alms to the poor, was instructed to send for Peter who would declare to him words "whereby thou shalt be saved" (11:14). Fourth, we learn

---

[20]Peter did not repeat his sermon; he rested his defense not on what he said but on what God did.
[21]"At the beginning" (v. 15) may imply that there had been no tongues-speaking since Pentecost.

that when people act on the light which God has given them, they may expect God to give them more light.

IV. THE WORK OF BARNABAS (11:19-30).

We are treating this paragraph as a part of the larger section of Acts (8:4—12:25) which concerns the witness in Judea and Samaria. The actual locale of the present narrative, however, was Antioch, which (along with its suburbs) boasted 800,000 inhabitants. The story of the work at Antioch was obviously inserted at this point in order to prepare us for the narrative of the larger mission to the Gentile world, which is the dominant theme of chapters 13-28. The present account, for instance, points up the importance of the city of Antioch, showing that large-scale and organized evangelization of the Gentiles was first undertaken in that city. Furthermore, it informs us that Saul of Tarsus, as well as Barnabas, was associated with this new development. And finally, it is made clear that the whole movement was looked upon with favor by the Jerusalem church, despite misgivings referred to in 11:2 and (later) in 15:1-5.

The third largest city of the Empire (surpassed only by Rome and Alexandria), Antioch was popularly known as "The Queen of the East," "Antioch the Beautiful," and "Antioch the Great." It was situated on the Orontes River about fifteen or twenty miles from Seleucia, its seaport.

Antioch was founded by Seleucus Nicator in 300 B.C. and served as the capital city of the Seleucid monarchy. When Syria, in 64 B.C., became a part of the Roman Empire, Antioch was made a free city (having its own municipal government) and the seat of the provincial administration of Syria. The population was mainly Syrian, but in language and culture the city was Greek. Like Rome and Alexandria, Antioch had a large Jewish community. The moral corruption of the city was notorious. For example, when the satirist Juvenal wanted to sum up the degredation of Rome, he complained that "the sewage of the Syrian Orontes has for long been discharged into the Tiber." Antioch was therefore "a field white for the harvest 'grasping like a thirsty land' for a renovating and life-giving gospel; and the large fringe of Gentile adherents which hung round the synagogue offered the Christian evangelist a golden opportunity" (Rackham, p. 165).

Antioch is the center of interest (apart from the episode of 12:1-23) in the story of Acts from this point (11:19) through chapter 14. The narrative contains three movements: the evangelization of Antioch (11:19-26), the collection at Antioch (11:27-

79

30), and the launching of the first missionary journey of Barnabas and Saul from Antioch (chs. 13, 14).

Antioch eventually superseded Jerusalem as the center of Christianity and became famous as the seat of a school of theology. Among the honorable names associated with the church at Antioch are Ignatius and John Chrysostom.

There have been two previous references to Barnabas in Acts: in 4:36, 37, where it is recorded that he sold a field which belonged to him and brought the money and laid it at the apostles' feet for distribution to the needy in the church; and in 9:27, where we are told that he befriended Saul when everyone else in the Jerusalem church was afraid of him and did not believe that he was a disciple. Here again he is seen living up to his name: "son of encouragement."

The paragraph divides itself into three parts: (1) the founding of the church at Antioch (vv. 19-21), (2) Barnabas' mission to Antioch (vv. 22-26), and (3) the benevolence of the church at Antioch (vv. 27-30).

1. *The founding of the church at Antioch (vv. 19-21).* Beginning with the story of Philip's work (ch. 8), each incident recorded thus far by Luke has led toward a Gospel free from Jewish limitations. The present passage represents the final step toward a definite program based on this principle.

Verse 19, which opens with the same words which introduce 8:4, takes us back to that point of departure. In 8:4 it is stated that those who were scattered abroad following the death of Stephen "went everywhere preaching the word." The narrative of 8:4b—11:18 has told us of those who preached within Palestine. The present verse informs us that there were some — "unnamed, unknown, unsung heroes" — who went beyond Palestine. They "traveled as far as Phoenicia, and Cyprus, and Antioch, speaking the word to none save only to Jews" (v. 19b, ASV). "Phoenicia," on the shore of the Mediterranean just west and north of Galilee, corresponds to modern Lebanon. About a hundred and twenty miles long and fifteen miles wide, its principal cities in the biblical era were Tyre, Sidon, Byblus, and Tripolis. In New Testament times Phoenicia formed part of the Roman province of Syria. The Christian communities founded in Phoenicia are referred to in Acts 21:4 and 27:3. "Cyprus," the easternmost of the larger islands of the Mediterranean, lies nearly opposite Antioch. In terms of today's world, it is sixty miles west of the coast of Syria, forty miles south of the coast of Turkey. In early times it was famous for its copper. The English word in fact is derived from the Greek name of the island *(Kypros)* through the Latin *(Cuprum).* Its main cities were Citium, Salamis, and Paphos. Cyprus is mentioned elsewhere in the Bible only in Acts 13:4; 15:39; 21:3; and 27:4. Cypriotes (i.e, men of Cyprus) are referred to in Acts 4:36; 11:20; and 21:16. "Antioch," one of the largest, wealthiest, and most luxurious cities of the empire, is discussed above. "At the time of its evangelization it was said to have been composed of four cities, each with its own surrounding wall. Reaching around the whole was a long wall which enclosed more area than the city of Rome. The four cities were separated by the two main streets of Antioch" (Carter and Earle, p. 156). Daphne, a center for the worship of Apollo and Artemis, was only five miles away and contributed greatly to the city's reputation for lax sexual morals.

These first witnesses to the areas mentioned spoke the word "only to Jews" (v. 19b, ASV). "But there were some of them, men of Cyprus and Cyrene, who, when they were come to Antioch, spake unto the Greeks also, preaching the Lord Jesus" (v. 20, ASV). Haenchen speaks of this as opening "a new chapter — and in a sense the most important — in the history of the Christian mission" (p. 366). There are at least four things to be observed in this verse: First, it speaks of preaching to "the Greeks" *(Hellenas),* not "Grecians" *(Hellenistas,* KJV). The "Greeks" were Gentiles; "Grecians" were Greek-speaking Jews (cf. 6:1).[22] This then was an instance of the·Gospel being preached to Gentiles entirely independent of that recorded in chapter 10 (the Cornelius episode). Whether it occurred before or after Peter preached to Cornelius' household, we cannot know. Perhaps the placing of the narrative after that about Cornelius is intended to suggest that the preaching referred to in this verse followed that to Cornelius. Second, this preaching was at Antioch, the largest pagan city to which the dispersed Christians had yet gone. Third, the preaching was done by "men of Cyprus and Cyrene." This means, of course, that they (like Stephen and Philip) were Hellenists (i.e., Grecian Jews). Bruce calls them "daring spirits" who "took a momentous step forward" (pp. 238, 239). Cyrene (cf. Matt. 27:32; Acts 2:10; 6:9; 13:1), which had a large Jewish population, was a province

---

22The Greek text is doubtful, some manuscripts containing the word *Hellenas* ("Greeks") and others having the word *Hellenistas* ("Grecians"). The majority of manuscripts support the latter reading, but the context requires the former. The writer obviously represents the preaching to this group as something new and remarkable — an advance in the Christian witness. In light of this, Lake and Cadbury, Bruce, and others feel that if *Hellenistas* is accepted as the correct reading it must here be interpreted in its wider sense of "Greek-speaking," including Greek-speaking Gentiles as well as Greek-speaking Jews.

in North Africa. Fourth, the substance of their preaching was "the Lord Jesus." This was the appropriate approach to Gentiles, for they, being ignorant of the hope of Israel, could not have understood the concept of messiahship. The Greek words for Lord *(kurios)* and Savior *(soter),* however, "were widely current in the religious world of the eastern Mediterranean" (Bruce, p. 239).

Verse 21 reports that the new work met with great success, a fact apparently brought in as an indication of the approval of God. "The hand of the Lord" is perhaps a "Semitic expression for the power of the Lord" (Carter and Earle, p. 157), though Lake and Cadbury understand it as simply a circumlocution for God (p. 129). The particle which connects the two parts of verse 21 is one which shows close connection, suggesting that it was because the power of the Lord was with the disciples that "a great number believed and turned to the Lord." There had been remarkable manifestations of God's saving power on earlier occasions — the eunuch, Cornelius, etc. — but nothing on the scale of the evangelization of Gentiles in Antioch.

2. *The Mission of Barnabas (vv. 22-26).* The mission of Barnabas to Antioch was similar to that of Peter and John to Samaria at an earlier time (ch. 8). In both instances the work had taken a new direction, and the Jerusalem church felt that caution was in order.

The *occasion* for Barnabas' mission is set out in verse 22. In a word, it was the report reaching Jerusalem of the success attending the work among Gentiles in Antioch. "When word of it came to the attention of the Jerusalem church, they sent Barnabas to Antioch" *(Modern Language).* The relatively mild reaction of the Jerusalem church to the news of the conversion of Gentiles at Antioch (cf. the astonishment of Peter and his companions in the house of Cornelius) is an indication that this episode came later than that which centered about Cornelius. That Barnabas, a man of broad sympathies and (like some of the preachers in Antioch) a native of Cyprus, was selected for this work "shows that no captious spirit was behind the move, and that he did not return to report and get formal sanction of his decision shows both the full confidence in him and the general spirit of local freedom already arising" (Carver, p. 123). In the ASV the last part of this verse reads: "and they sent forth Barnabas *as far as Antioch."* This rendering suggests that he was to investigate the work all the way in Antioch, but it is reasonable to suppose that the city of Antioch was the principal point of his concern.

The *response* of Barnabas (vv. 23, 24) was such that it must have cheered the believers in Antioch. There is no indication that he altered or amended any part of the work. Recognizing at once that it was of the Lord, he gave it his endorsement and rejoiced. Goodspeed: "When he reached there and saw the favor God had shown them, he was delighted" (v. 23a). And, true to his name ("son of encouragement"), "he encouraged them all to be resolute and steadfast in their devotion to the Lord" (v. 23b, Goodspeed). Weymouth: "he encouraged them all to remain, with fixed resolve, faithful to the Lord." The Greek verb for "encouraged," in the imperfect tense, suggests a repeated or continuous action. To be "resolute and steadfast" in devotion to the Lord is to persevere in loyalty to Him. "Antioch," writes Lindsay, "was full of temptations, and sin must have had strong hold on the bodies of men who had been heathens there; nothing but keeping in the closest possible communion with the Lord Jesus could avail" (I, 127).

Such a response from Barnabas was to be expected, for he was a man of sterling character — " a good man, and full of the Holy Spirit and of faith" (v. 24a, ASV). "Good" renders a word which means good in nature and here probably suggests a benevolent disposition. "Full of the Holy Spirit" should be compared with the description of Stephen in 6:5. Barnabas' coming was a stimulus to the work: "and a great number of people were brought to the Lord" (v. 24b, NIV).

Verses 25 and 26 tell of Barnabas' search for an assistant. The demands of the work were so great that he could not possibly handle it alone; he therefore set about to find a colleague who might help him. His thoughts turned to Saul of Tarsus, who had for several years now been in Tarsus (cf. 9:30). No man was more eminently suited for the type of work which was needed in Antioch. Indeed, he was especially chosen of God for work among the Gentiles (cf. 9:15) — a fact of which Barnabas could hardly have been ignorant. Barnabas therefore "went forth to Tarsus to seek for Saul" (v. 25, ASV). The Greek word for "seek," used only by Luke in the New Testament (cf. Luke 2:44, 45), denotes effort and thoroughness, a looking up and down. The idea is that Barnabas did not know at what precise place Saul was to be found, only that he was in Tarsus. Bruce thinks Saul had been "disinherited for his Christian confession and could no longer be found at his ancestral home" (p. 240). In time he "found him" and "brought him unto Antioch" (v. 26a, ASV). "The hour and the man met when Barnabas brought Saul to Antioch" (Robertson, p. 159). For an entire year they met with the church and taught the people.

"They assembled themselves with the church" (v. 26) is variously interpreted. Rieu: "joining in the worship of the church"; Weymouth: "they were guests of the church." Hort's rendering is similar to Weymouth's: "they were hospitably received in the church" (quoted by Knowling, p. 268).

Luke adds, almost as an afterthought, that "the disciples were called Christians first in Antioch" (v. 26b). The name was given them by Gentiles, for Jews would not have given even this tacit approval to the messiahship of Jesus. It may have been given to distinguish believers from Jews, with whose religion Christianity had much in common. Some think the name was used as a term of derision (cf. Acts 26:28; 1 Peter 4:16), but that may not have been so in Antioch. Probably the name arose from the fact that believers were always talking about one whom they called "the Christ." They thus came to be known as "the Christ-people," "Christians." Until this time Christians were known as disciples, believers, brothers, saints, followers of the Way, etc., and it was by these names that they continued to designate themselves.

3. *The benevolence of the church at Antioch (vv. 27-30).* The paragraph closes with a touching account of the benevolence of the congregation at Antioch. During the period in which Barnabas and Saul were ministering to the church, "there came down prophets [i.e., persons speaking for God under the immediate inspiration of the Holy Spirit; cf. 1 Cor. 12:28; 14:29ff.; Eph. 2:20; 4:11; Acts 15:32][23] from Jerusalem unto Antioch" (v. 27, ASV). Among these prophets there was a man "named Agabus" (mentioned also in Acts 21:10), who "signified by the Spirit that there should be a great famine over all the world"[24] (v. 28a, ASV). Luke adds that this prediction actually "came to pass in the days of Claudius," who was emperor from A.D. 44 to 54. From other sources we know that Claudius' reign was marked by frequent famine. Josephus, for instance, writes of famine conditions in Judea between A.D. 44 and 49. At any rate, the believers of Antioch took seriously the words of Agabus and "determined to send relief unto the brethren that dwelt in Judaea" (v. 29, ASV). Everyone gave "according to his ability" (v. 29a; cf. 1 Cor. 16:2), and all that was contributed was sent to the elders by the hand of Barnabas and Saul"[25] (v. 30, ASV). "Elders," who are mentioned here for the first time as officebearers

---

[23]The function of the prophets of New Testament times was to give instruction and guidance to the people of God.

[24]The Greek word is *oikoumene,* which was used to denote the "inhabited world," that is, "the Roman world."

[25]Many interpreters think this is the visit which Paul describes in Galatians 2:1-10, but traditionally that visit has been identified with the visit recorded in Acts 15.

in the church, were Christian preachers.[26] Here they are seen doing the type of work for which the Seven were earlier selected (cf. 6:1ff.).

We should perhaps think of this visit of Barnabas and Saul as occurring some time after the events recorded in Acts 12:1-23. Some think the visit came as much as a year or two after Herod's death. Bruce suggests A.D. 46, two years after the king's death, as the most probable date. Haenchen, on the other hand, thinks Luke intends us to understand that Barnabas and Saul arrived in Jerusalem about the time of James' death, and that they stayed throughout the critical period. It was "on this account," he says, "that they entrusted their gift to the elders, not to the Apostles, who were being persecuted and were on the run" (p. 64).

The bounty which they brought from the Gentile congregation at Antioch was in itself an effective report on the character of the work which Barnabas more than a year before had been sent to investigate.

Three "new" things emerge from this episode narrated in 11:19-30: a new center for missionary work (Antioch), a new name for disciples (Christians), and a new team for spreading the Gospel (Barnabas and Saul).

V. THE PERSECUTION OF HEROD (12:1-25).

Six members of the Herod family appear in the biblical records as rulers: (1) Herod the Great, king of the Jews at the time of Jesus' birth; (2) Archelaus (called "Herod the Ethnarch" on his coins), who reigned in Judea "in the room of his father Herod" (Matt. 2:22) from 4 B.C. to A.D. 6 but never was given the title "king"; (3) "Herod the tetrarch" (Luke 3:19, etc.), a son of Herod the Great who was known also as Antipas and was the ruler under whom John the Baptist was executed; (4) Philip (Luke 3:1), another son of Herod the Great; (5) "Herod the king" (Acts 12:1), who was sometimes called "Herod Agrippa I" and was a son of Aristobulus and grandson of Herod the Great; and (6) Agrippa (Acts 25:13—26:32), son of "Herod the king."

Upon the death of Herod the Great (4 B.C.), the kingdom over which he ruled was divided among three of his sons: *Philip* became tetrarch of Iturea, the country north and east of the Sea of Galilee, and reigned until A.D. 34. *Herod Antipas* was made tetrarch of Galilee and Perea and ruled until A.D. 39, when he was recalled by Rome for a suspected plot against the emperor's life. *Archelaus*

---

[26]A comparison of Acts 20:17, 28; Titus 1:5, 7 appears to show that "bishop" and "elder" were terms used, at least in some instances, interchangeably.

became ethnarch of Judea (which included both Samaria and Idumea). He was deposed in A.D. 6 and banished to Gaul. At this time Judea was made a part of the province of Syria and was governed by procurators until A.D. 41. In A.D. 41 the whole of Palestine passed under the rule of Herod Agrippa I, who, following the execution of his father in 7 B.C., was brought up in Rome in close association with the imperial family. He continued as ruler of all Palestine until his death in A.D. 44. By deferring to Jewish scruples and observing Jewish regulations he won the favor of the people and was looked upon by them as a successful ruler. This is the "Herod" of the passage now under consideration.

The events of this chapter may be accurately dated, for it is known from extra-biblical records that the death of Herod (referred to in 12:23) occurred in A.D. 44. The passage is an important one, then, in determining the chronology of the Book of Acts.

The chapter may be divided into four parts: (1) the execution of James (vv. 1, 2), (2) the attempt on the life of Peter (vv. 3-19), (3) the outcome of Herod's persecutions (vv. 20-24), and (4) the return of Barnabas and Saul to Antioch (v. 25).

1. *The execution of James (vv. 1, 2).* The James of these verses is the apostle, son of Zebedee, brother of John. "About that time" (lit., "at that time"; v. 1), a phrase which connects this narrative with that of the preceding chapter, places his arrest and execution at about the time of the gathering of the offering at Antioch for the believers of Judea. Carver conjectures that it fell between the events of 11:27-29 and the sending of the offering by the hands of Barnabas and Saul (11:30).

The Greek word for "vex" (v. 1b) means to injure, to afflict, to impose hardship upon. "Certain of the church" (v. 1b) shows that the persecution referred to extended to a number of believers, how many we do not know. James is mentioned specifically, partly because of his prominence in the church and partly because in his case persecution resulted in martyrdom. Reference to his being killed "with the sword" (v. 2) suggests that he was beheaded (cf. Weymouth).

Carver thinks it remarkable that so little space is given to the martyrdom of an apostle. "Men were not glorified in the early church; and death was put in its proper place of relative insignificance in the Christian system and thought" (p. 129).

2. *The attempt on the life of Peter (vv. 3-19).* Seeing that the execution of James gratified the Jews, Herod went further and arrested Peter also. If the murder of James pleased the Jews, thought Herod, how much more favor he could win for himself by

putting the chief of the apostles out of the way! After all, Peter had on a number of occasions been a brother to the Jewish leaders.

Verses 3 and 4 vividly describe *the arrest and imprisonment* (the third for Peter; cf. 4:3; 5:18). It occurred at the time of the festival of unleavened bread. (Probably the reference is to the entire period of the Passover feast, 14th to 21st Nisan.) The apostle was put in prison and entrusted to the keeping of sixteen soldiers (i.e., a squad of soldiers relieved four times a day). The intention was to "produce him in public after the Passover" (NEB).

Verses 5-9 describe in minute detail *Peter's deliverance.* The account emphasizes five things: (1) the timeliness of the deliverance ("On the very night before Herod had planned to bring him forward"; v. 5, NEB); (2) the maximum security of the imprisonment (between two soldiers, v. 6; bound with two chains, v. 6; guards before the door, v. 6; an iron gate, v. 10); (3) the passivity of Peter (sleeping, v. 6; chains falling from his hands, v. 7; submissively obeying repeated commands by the angel: rise up, v. 7; gird thyself, v. 8; bind on thy sandals, v. 8; cast thy garment about thee and follow me, v. 8); (4) the prayer of the church (vv. 5b, 12b); and (5) the surprise of the church when Peter was delivered and their reluctance to believe that it had really happened (vv. 15, 16). From this last fact it would appear that the prayers of the church were lacking in faith, but God often gives us more than we expect and always more than we deserve.

After this episode, Herod left Jerusalem and went back to Caesarea, which was the seat of government and his permanent residence.

3. *The outcome of Herod's persecutions (vv. 20-24).* Two things are mentioned:

(1) *Divine judgment on Herod* (vv. 20-23). A question of politics now engages Herod's attention. "Tyre and Sidon," cities of Phoenicia, were dependent upon Herod's realm for their food supply (cf. v. 20b). When, therefore, they became aware that they had offended Herod — by what means we do not know — they sent a deputation to wait on him. When the deputation arrived in Caesarea, they won over Blastus the king's treasurer (perhaps by bribery) and had him arrange a meeting with Herod so that they might beg him to be friendly with them again (v. 20). On an appointed day[27] the king, arrayed in royal apparel, took his seat on the rostrum and made a public address (v. 21). The audience,

---

[27]Josephus, who describes the occasion, says it was on the second day of a festival in honor of Caesar. The royal apparel, he explains, included a robe made of silver thread.

eager to flatter the king, shouted, "It is a god's voice, not a man's!" (v. 22, Moffatt). At that moment the angel of the Lord struck him, "because he had usurped the honour due to God" (v. 23a, NEB). Becoming worm-eaten, he died.[28] The year was A.D. 44.

The position of this account in Luke's narrative seems to imply that the sacred writer wanted to show some connection between the death of Herod and the earlier persecutions of Christians which he had instigated.

(2) *Growth of the Word of God* (v. 24). Occasional summary statements are a characteristic feature of the Book of Acts (cf. 6:7; 9:31). Verse 24 is such a summary. It presents a vivid contrast: the tyrant, eaten by worms, dies (v. 23); "but the word of God grew and multiplied" (v. 24). "Gave up the ghost" (v. 23), translating an aorist tense (point action), signifies the death of opposition. "Grew" and "multiplied" are both present tenses and speak of the continuing growth, etc., of the word. "Meanwhile the Lord's Message kept extending, and spreading far and wide" (TCNT).

4. *The return of Barnabas and Saul to Antioch (v. 25).*[29] Having performed their mission to Jerusalem in behalf of the Antioch church (cf. 11:30), Barnabas and Saul returned to the city on the Orontes, taking with them John Mark (the cousin of Barnabas, Col. 4:10).[30] All things were now ready for launching a great missionary thrust into the Gentile world.

FOR FURTHER STUDY

1. Make a list of the conversions recorded in Acts and compare the accounts.

2. Read and compare the three Acts accounts of Paul's conversion (Acts 9; 22; 26).

3. Read Galatians 1:11-24 and show how the incidents related there fit into the narrative of Acts 9.

4. Using a map of Palestine, trace the missionary journeys of Peter.

---

[28]Josephus, giving details which supplement the biblical record, says Herod was smitten one day and died five days later.

[29]The Greek text of verse 25 is somewhat confusing. The best-attested reading is *"to* Jerusalem," but the sense of the verse requires *"from* Jerusalem." Goodspeed resolves the matter by rendering: "When Barnabas and Saul had performed their mission to Jerusalem, they went back, taking John who was called Mark with them."

[30]In light of Mark's being enlisted at this time, it may be reasonable to suppose that Barnabas and Saul had lodged in his mother's home while they were in Jerusalem (cf. Bruce, p. 258).

5. Make a list of the personal names appearing in Acts 12.

6. Read articles in a Bible dictionary on Philip; Eunuch; Paul; Peter; Cornelius; Barnabas.

CHAPTER 4

Witness in Cyprus and Central Asia Minor

(Acts 13:1—14:28)

At this point Luke's narrative of the third phase of the Christian witness is begun (cf. 1:8): Acts 1:1—8:3 has described the witness in Jerusalem; 8:4—12:25, the witness in all Judea and Samaria; chapters 13 through 28 will now tell how the Gospel was taken beyond Palestine to Rome itself. Up to this point, though there have been notable exceptions (the eunuch, Cornelius and his household, and the people of Antioch), the Christian witness has been decidedly Jewish; and the chief center for the dissemination of the Gospel has been Jerusalem. Beginning with chapter 13, the emphasis is essentially on Gentile work; and the base of operation is seen to be Antioch rather than Jerusalem. Indeed, the shift from Jerusalem to Antioch was seen to be in the making in 11:19-30.

Another change is to be observed. Peter, who has dominated the story throughout the first twelve chapters, appears only briefly in chapters 13 through 28; indeed, after chapter 15 he is not mentioned a single time. On the other hand, Paul, who was introduced almost incidentally in the account of the martyrdom of Stephen, whose conversion and early work were described at length in chapter 9, and whose association with Barnabas was briefly noticed in 11:25-30 and 12:25, will now almost completely dominate the story of Acts.

The passage now to be considered (chs. 13 and 14) may be divided into two unequal parts: (1) the call of Barnabas and Saul to missionary service (13:1-3) and (2) the missionary journey of Barnabas and Saul (13:4—14:28).

I. THE CALL OF BARNABAS AND SAUL TO MISSIONARY SERVICE (13:1-3).

Barnabas and Saul, bringing with them John Mark, now returned to Antioch (cf. 12:25). And it is here that the Holy Spirit calls them to a new work. Luke, in describing the call and its circumstances, emphasizes the leadership of the church at the time (v. 1), the activity in which they were engaged (v. 2), and the action by which Barnabas and Saul were formally set apart (v. 3).

1. *The leadership of the church (v. 1).* This consisted of "prophets and teachers." It is debated whether Luke is describing two offices (i.e., some of the persons named being prophets, others teachers) or two functions exercised by all of the persons listed. Some interpreters (Ramsay, e.g.) argue that the insertion of the Greek particle *te* before Manaen's name suggests two offices. If this line of interpretation is followed, the first three persons in the list (Barnabas, Symeon, and Lucius) are prophets; the last two (Manaen and Saul), teachers. Lake and Cadbury, on the other hand, doubt the Greek particle "can quite bear the strain of this interpretation," adding that Saul was surely "quite as much a prophet as Barnabas" (p. 141). We may conclude that Ramsay's suggestion, while attractive, is too subtle to be conclusive.

"Prophets" were men inspired of the Holy Spirit to speak a message for God (cf. Acts 2:17; 11:27; 1 Cor. 12:28; 14:1-5). They ranked next to apostles in order of importance in apostolic churches. "Teachers," mentioned here for the first time in Acts, also played a prominent role in the leadership of apostolic churches. In 1 Corinthians 12:28 they are ranked immediately after apostles and prophets. Their work was to give believers instruction in the practical duties of the Christian life and to ground them in knowledge of the Old Testament and the teachings of Jesus.

The listing of the names of the five prophets and teachers is of considerable interest. For instance, there may be significance in the fact that Barnabas is listed first; this may reflect that he was the most prominent and influential man of the group. (We should hesitate to conclude, however, that the placing of Saul's name last suggests that he was the least prominent of the group.) Again, the Greek may suggest that the names fall into two groups: Barnabas, Symeon, and Lucius in one group, Manaen and Saul making up the second. Why they are grouped in this fashion we cannot know. Finally, for Barnabas and Saul, who have already been introduced to us, there are no descriptive phrases. For each of the others, however, there is such a phrase. Symeon, we are told, was "called Niger." This was a Latin nickname meaning "black," "dark-complexioned." Bruce wonders whether he was identical with Simon of Cyrene who carried the cross of Jesus, but in the absence of any positive proof he stops short of making this identification.

Lucius is said to be "of Cyrene" (a province in North Africa; cf. 11:20). A few interpreters are inclined to identify him with Luke, but most think this is improbable. It was a common name in the Roman world. Manaen (Greek for the Hebrew "Menahem") is said to be "the foster-brother of Herod the tetrarch" (ASV). The Greek word for "foster-brother" was a title of honor "given to boys of the same age as royal princes, who were brought up with them at court" (Bruce, p. 260). Lake and Cadbury render it "companion" (p. 142); *Modern Language,* "a childhood companion"; RSV, "a member of the court." Carver suggests that Manaen's mother may have been the royal nurse. The Herod to whom Manaen was foster brother was Herod Antipas, son of Herod the Great and murderer of John the Baptist.

Lumby comments on the list as follows: "One a Cypriote, another a Cyrenian, another a Jew, but from his double name accustomed to mix among non-Jews, one a connection of the Idumean house of Herod, and Saul the heaven-appointed apostle to the Gentiles, the list may be deemed in some sort typical of 'all the world,' into which the gospel was now to go forth."

2. *The activity in which they were engaged (v. 2a).* It was as they ministered to the Lord and fasted that the Spirit spoke to them. "Ministered" is the translation of a verb which in the Septuagint is used of the official service of priests and Levites. Used only three times in the New Testament (here; Rom. 15:27; Heb. 10:11), it probably speaks in the present passage of "the ministry of public worship" (Knowling, p. 282). Fasting was an indication of intense earnestness. Carter and Earle understand the verb as emphasizing "a state of uninterrupted concentration which made it possible to ascertain the will of the Lord" (p. 175). Carver wonders "whether these men were thinking eagerly of new fields for gospel expansion" (p. 136).

We are not told how the Spirit made His will known. Knowling thinks "we may reasonably infer by one of the prophets." The two men whom He designated, Barnabas and Saul, were probably the most outstanding leaders in the church. Earlier the Spirit had brought the two together and to Antioch (11:19ff.), doubtless with this moment in mind.

The call of the Spirit referred to here marks a new departure. Up to this time the diffusion of the Gospel had been accomplished chiefly through the witness of refugees. But now men are to be set apart for the specific purpose of telling the good news where it has not been heard.

3. *The act by which they were set apart (v. 3).* It was after "they

had prayed and fasted" that "they laid hands on" Barnabas and Saul and "sent them away." "They" has as its logical antecedent the "prophets and teachers" of verse 1, but we may well suppose that the whole church was in some way involved in this experience. The laying on of hands should not be thought of as ordination to the ministry. Both of these men had been for many years engaged in the work of ministry. Nor should we think of it as a setting apart to the office of apostle. Apostles were appointed by God, not men. The office of apostle "was a status which the church could not bestow but only recognize" (Bruce, p. 261). It is best to think of the laying on of hands in this instance as a symbolic act in which the church recognized the divine call of Barnabas and Saul, expressed its fellowship with them, and sent them forth with its blessing.

From verses 1-3 the following principles may be derived: (1) Opportunities for greater service ordinarily come not to the idle but to those who are faithfully performing their present duties. (2) When God calls someone to a task, He often will make this known not only to the recipient of the call but to others as well. (3) Churches should be willing to part with the very best in their membership for the greater diffusion of the Gospel. (4) Churches should enlarge their vision, being mindful not only of the needs immediately about them but also of the needs of the whole world. (There were more than half a million pagans in Antioch, but God wanted two of His choicest servants to go to fields abroad.)

II. THE MISSIONARY JOURNEY OF BARNABAS AND SAUL (13:4—14:28).

This first missionary journey covered a period of approximately two years, from about A.D. 46 to A.D. 47 or 48. (Carver says the journey lasted from one to three years, falling within the years A.D. 45 and 48; Haenchen does not mention a beginning date, but has it close before A.D. 48; Ogg puts the beginning of the journey early in A.D. 46 and the return to Antioch late in 47.)

That Barnabas, at the beginning of the journey, was leader may be inferred from the order of the names at the outset: "Barnabas and Saul." Before the journey was completed, however, the order is reversed, suggesting that Saul had assumed the ascendant role.

1. *The outward journey (13:4—14:20).* The opening words of verse 4, "So they, being sent forth by the Holy Spirit," are strikingly similar to the closing words of verse 3: "they [the church] sent them away." The suggestion is that the Holy Spirit was the ultimate agent in sending forth the missionaries. The church acted only as His instrument. Lindsay comments: "This first missionary

journey had its origin in 'a combination of the human and the Divine'; it was the joint work of the Church and of the Holy Ghost. Every work for Christ is a partnership with God" (II, 43).

The places visited on this journey were the following:

(1) *Seleucia* (13:4a). Built (301 B.C.) by and named for Seleucus Nicator, the first king of the Seleucid dynasty, Seleucia served as seaport of Antioch. It was located about sixteen miles from Antioch and five miles north of the mouth of the Orontes River. No mention is made of preaching here, the only statement being that the missionaries "went down to Seleucia" and from thence "sailed to Cyprus."

(2) *Cyprus* (13:4b-12). The county of Barnabas' birth, Cyprus is the largest island in the eastern Mediterranean. At an earlier time it had been colonized by Phoenicians and Greeks and had been successively ruled by Assyrian, Persian, Ptolemaic, and Roman empires. At the time of our narrative it was under Roman domination. Though the island had a large Jewish community, its population was mainly Greek.

It should be borne in mind that the witness of Barnabas and Saul was not the first which Cyprus had heard. It had already been visited by some of the Christian refugees who fled Jerusalem after the martyrdom of Stephen (cf. 11:19, 20).

The missionaries traversed the entire island (v. 6a), but Luke mentions specifically the work in its two principal cities: Salamis (v. 5) and Paphos (vv. 6b-12). The former, the site of which is three miles north of modern Famagusta, on the east side of the island, was at one time the chief city of Cyprus. In New Testament times it was a flourishing commercial center and the chief seat of government for Eastern Cyprus. Luke mentions only two things in reference to the work in Salamis: the missionaries preached in "the synagogues of the Jews," and they had John Mark "as their attendant" (v. 5, ASV). "Attendant" is the translation of a Greek word (cf. Luke 4:20; 1 Cor. 4:1) which was used of any doer of hard work; from this it came to denote one who does service to another, that is, "a helper," "assistant," "servant," "underling," etc. In Athens it was used of the servant who attended each man-at-arms, carrying his baggage, rations, shield, etc. Zenophon used it of men who were in attendance on a general, as aides-de-camp or adjutants. Lindsay thinks it here suggests that Mark waited on Barnabas and Saul, aiding them in preaching and perhaps baptizing for them (cf. 1 Cor. 1:13-16). In general, we may think of Mark doing whatever was necessary to give the apostles greater freedom for the work of evangelizing.

Paphos was the name of two settlements in southwest Cyprus, designated by scholars as Old Paphos and New Paphos. The former, a Phoenician settlement of great antiquity, lay about a mile inland. New Paphos, which is the city meant in the text, was about seven miles northwest of Old Paphos. New Paphos, by New Testament times, had superseded the old town and was the provincial capital and residence of the Roman governor. Both Old Paphos and New Paphos were notoriously wicked, being centers for the worship of Aphrodite.

Three significant occurrences at Paphos are recorded: (a) the encounter with Bar-Jesus, described in verse 6 as "a certain sorcerer, a false prophet, a Jew";[1] (b) the conversion[2] of Sergius Paulus the proconsul, described in verse 7 as "a man of understanding"; and (c) the shift from the use of the Jewish name "Saul" to the Roman "Paul" (v. 9). It was customary for Jews to bear two names, one Hebrew and one Roman. Paul therefore probably bore both names from birth. Perhaps he began to use "Paul" at this point because his work was taking him more and more into contact with Gentiles. It is probably only a coincidence that the proconsul was also named Paul. "Filled with the Spirit" should be compared with 4:8, where the same assertion is made of Peter. Lindsay thinks of the experience here as "a sudden inspiration making Paul see the earnestness of the proconsul, and the evil temptings of Bar-Jesus, and giving him power to rebuke miraculously" (II, 45).

(3) *Perga* (13:13). The next province to be visited by the missionaries was Pamphylia, which lay on the south coast of Asia Minor. Perga, the ruins of which are at modern Murtana in Turkey, was its capital. The city lay twelve miles inland from Attalia (modern Antalya), where the missionary party probably landed. In connection with the visit to Perga two things are to be observed: (a) From this point on Paul assumes the leadership of the group (note: "Paul and his company"). Furneaux (quoted by Robertson) writes: "In nothing is the greatness of Barnabas more manifest than in his recognition of the superiority of Paul and acceptance of a secondary position for himself." (b) John Mark leaves the mis-

---

[1] In verse 8 he is called "Elymas the sorcerer," with the explanation that this is "his name by interpretation." It is thought that "Elymas" is the Greek form of a Semitic (Arabic) word meaning something like sorcerer.

[2] The proconsul, according to verse 7b, requested Barnabas and Saul to explain to him the word of God. In verse 12, after the infliction of blindness on Elymas, it is said that Sergius Paulus "believed." If taken in its full sense, this means he was converted; and though his baptism is not mentioned, it is then implied. Some interpreters do not think the proconsul was truly converted. Lake and Cadbury, for instance, think the missionaries "may have mistaken courtesy for conversion."

sionaries and returns to Jerusalem. It is idle to speculate on the reason for this, though Paul apparently felt the action was blameworthy (cf. 15:38). It has been suggested by some that Mark resented the assumption by Paul of leadership of the missionary party.

(4) *Pisidian Antioch* (13:14-52). The apostles appear to have left Perga shortly after they arrived. Ramsay suggests it was because the area was low and infested with malaria. Antioch, across the Taurus mountains, was north of Perga and in much higher country. It was not *in* Pisidia (KJV) but was known as Antioch "of" Pisidia (or Antioch "toward" Pisidia) because it was near the border of Pisidia. Actually located in the region known as Galatic Phrygia, Antioch was made a part of the Roman province of Galatia in 25 B.C. A short while later, in 6 B.C., it was made a colony (like Philippi), and as such became the administrative and military center for its part of the province of Galatia.

Paul's first preaching in Antioch was in the synagogue, to the Jews, and it was at the invitation of "the rulers of the synagogue" (vv. 14b, 15).[3] The sermon delivered on this occasion, the first Pauline sermon which Luke has recorded, is given in verses 16-41. Three things are to be observed in reference to the sermon: First, it contains in germ some of the basic points of Paul's theology, for example, justification by faith and the inadequacy of the law for man's redemption. Second, the style of the message (a sort of historical summary) is quite similar to that of Stephen's address (ch. 7). Third, there is a note of joy and gladness which resounds in it (cf. "good tidings," v. 32; "the word of salvation," v. 26).

The message may be briefly outlined as follows: (a) *Introduction* (vv. 16-22). This takes the form of a brief sketch of Jewish history, culminating in David. (b) *Theme* (vv. 23-37). In this action Paul shows how the great messianic promise has been fulfilled in Jesus. The life and works are recounted in verses 23-25, His death in verses 27-29, His resurrection in verses 30-37. As in other sermons previously recorded in Acts, this one emphasizes that Jesus' resurrection was attested by eyewitnesses (vv. 30, 31) and Scripture (vv. 33-37). (c) *Conclusion* (vv. 38-41). At this point the apostle announces the promise of forgiveness and justification (vv. 38, 39)[4]

---

[3]Readings from both the law and the prophets were a regular part of the synagogue service. After the Scriptures were read, it was customary to have a message delivered (cf. Luke 4:16ff.). It was the responsibility of the "rulers" (NEB: "officials of the synagogue") to select readers and speakers for the service. Any rabbi or distinguished stranger might be called up to speak.

[4]Verse 39 states in succinct form the message of Galatians and Romans. The law, Paul affirms, could not justify, but Jesus can. It is not that He supplements the law; rather He achieves what it could not achieve (cf. Rom. 8:3).

and warns of the peril of rejecting the message of salvation (vv. 40, 41). Perhaps the warning was added because Paul saw anger in the eyes of some of those present.

Verses 42 and 43 describe *the effects* of the sermon: (a) The missionaries were earnestly begged to repeat all of this on the next Sabbath, the suggestion being that the audience recognized the message as unike anything which they had ever heard (v. 42). The KJV represents this request as coming from "the Gentiles," but these words are not in the best Greek text. The KJV also says that the request came "when the Jews were gone out of the synagogue." The ASV translates the better reading: "And as they [i.e., probably Paul and Barnabas] went out," suggesting that the missionaries left before the service was formally dismissed. (b) When the congregation was dismissed "many of the Jews and the devout proselytes [RSV, 'devout converts to Judaism'] followed Paul and Barnabas" (v. 43, ASV), apparently asking further questions of them. The two men, willing and glad to talk with them, "urged them to continue in the grace of God" (v. 43b, ASV).

The second stage of the witness in Antioch, narrated in verses 44-52, came a week later on a second Sabbath. During the intervening days those who had heard Paul in the synagogue on the first occasion spread the news so effectively that now "almost the whole city was gathered together to hear the word of God" (v. 44, ASV). The sight of such a multitude (composed of both Jews and Gentiles) assembled to hear the teaching of the missionaries filled the Jews with "jealous resentment" (v. 45a, NEB) and prompted them to keep "contradicting Paul's statements in violent language" (v. 45b, TCNT). Paul and Barnabas then announced that they were turning to the Gentiles (v. 46, 47).[5]

The Gentiles welcomed this turn of events, and the word of the Lord spread throughout the district to neighboring towns (vv. 48, 49). The Jews, however, inciting certain influential women[6] as well as the leading men of the town, stirred up a persecution against Paul and Barnabas. This resulted in their being driven out of the district (v. 50), but the disciples which they left in Antioch were

---

[5]Here we see a pattern which will characterize Paul's work in every area: The Gospel is preached first to the Jews and is joyfully received by some. But when objection is raised by the strict legalists, Paul turns to the Gentiles, and is welcomed by many of them.

[6]Perhaps they were wives of some of the leading citizens of the city. The Jews probably wanted them to influence their husbands to take action against the apostles. Bruce thinks they were "loosely attached to the synagogue as God-fearers."

"more and more filled with joy and with the Holy Spirit" (v. 52, Weymouth).

(5) *Iconium* (14:1-7). Described by Zenophon as the last city in Phrygia as one traveled east, Iconium was later united with Lycaonia in one district of Roman administration. It was a part of the larger Roman province of Galatia, and the church established by Paul and Barnabas in Iconium was probably among those churches to which Paul later addressed the Epistle to the Galatians. Iconium, ninety miles from Antioch, is now known as Konya (or Konia), a small Turkish town of 30,000 inhabitants.

As was their custom, the missionaries preached first in the synagogue; and their preaching was attended by great success: "a great multitude both of Jews and of Greeks believed" (v. 1b, ASV). Again, however, the Jews who refused to be persuaded of the truth of the Christian message "stirred up the Gentiles and poisoned their minds against the brethren" (v. 2b, RSV). They may have trumped up charges against the missionaries.

Paul and Barnabas, in spite of the opposition, continued to speak boldly in the Lord, and He authenticated their witness by "granting signs and wonders to be done by their hands" (v. 3, ASV). The people of the city were divided into parties, some siding with the Jews, some with the apostles (v. 4). Eventually, a movement was made on the part of both Jews and Gentiles, with the sanction of the authorities, "to mistreat and to stone them" (v. 5, NASB). The missionaries, having become aware of it, escaped to Lystra and Derbe, cities of Lycaonia. There they continued to preach the good news (vv. 6, 7). It was from this area that Timothy came.

(6) *Lystra* (14:8-20a). Located about eighteen miles south of Iconium, Lystra had been made a Roman colony by Augustus in 6 B.C. It was directly connected with Pisidian Antioch by a military road which bypassed Iconium. In Luke's account no mention is made of a synagogue, and from this we may infer that there were few Jews in the city and that Paul and Barnabas began their work by preaching to the Gentiles.

Two things of note are recorded: (a) a miracle performed by Paul (vv. 8-18) and (b) the stoning of Paul (vv. 19, 20a).

The *miracle* was performed on a man graphically described by Luke as "impotent in his feet, a cripple from his mother's womb, who never had walked" (v. 8, ASV). Paul, noticing the man in his audience, fastened his eyes on him and, when he perceived that the man had faith to be made whole, shouted to him: "Stand upright on thy feet" (vv. 9, 10a). At this, the man leaped up and began to walk (v. 10b). "It was a sudden spring as the faith found vent, one act showing that the cure was perfect (aorist tense), then a continuous power to walk (imperfect tense)" (Lindsay II, 55).

Seeing what Paul had done, the people "rent the air with their shouts" (v. 11a, Weymouth), crying out in their native Lycaonian speech: "The gods are come down to us in the likeness of men" (v. 11b). Barnabas, who was probably the older, more reserved of the two men, they called Jupiter (Greek, Zeus). (There was a temple dedicated to Jupiter which stood at the entrance of Lystra.) Recognizing Paul as the speaker, they called him Mercury (the messenger of the gods and spokesman for Jupiter) (v. 12). The priest of Jupiter soon appeared at the gate with oxen and garlands, intending to join the people in offering sacrifices (v. 13). That the gods sometimes assumed the shape of men and mingled among them was a common belief among the ancients. There was, in fact, a legend which said that Jupiter and Mercury once visited the people of Phrygia, a neighboring district.

Barnabas and Paul[7] probably did not understand the Lycaonian dialect, but upon inquiring about the cause of the commotion were told (note v. 14, "heard of it"). The response was a message, the second recorded sermon of this missionary journey. It is not clearly indicated whether the address was given by Paul or by Barnabas, but since Paul appears now as spokesman and leader we may assume that it was given by him. It is possible that Luke intends us to understand that this is the gist of what both men said. There was much confusion and excitement, and both may have been speaking. Remarkably similar to, though briefer than, the address at Athens recorded later (ch. 17), its subject is God. This was most appropriate in view of the fact that they had mistaken two preachers to be gods!

The message teaches that there is but one God, that He is a living God, and that He is Creator of all that exists (v. 15). Moreover, He guides the course of history and controls the destiny of men (v. 16).[8] The message closes with a reminder of God's goodness and grace (v. 17).

Nothing is said about conversions. We are simply told that even

[7]Notice that in verse 14 Barnabas is again named first, this apparently because he was looked upon as the chief god by the populace and accordingly took the lead on this occasion.

[8]The thought of verse 16 is that God's hand is upon all nations, but in the case of the Gentiles He in large measure withdrew His restraints as a judgment on them for their sins (cf. Acts 17:30; Rom. 1:24, 26, 28). Verse 17 shows, however, that even the Gentiles were dealt with in grace. God did not leave Himself "without witness" but "did good" to the Gentiles, giving them "rains and fruitful seasons" and filling their hearts with "food and gladness."

with words such as these the apostles were hardly able to keep the crowds from sacrificing to them (v. 18).

The *stoning* of Paul (vv. 19, 20a) was instigated by unbelieving Jews from Antioch and Iconium. Some think they were traveling merchants, others that they were simply hostile Jews who had purposely followed the missionaries. At any rate, they succeeded in turning the minds of the people against Paul, and the people stoned him and cast him out of their city for dead. (Luke does not say that Paul was dead, only that his oppressors supposed him to be dead. However, the beating was so serious and the recovery so sudden that the latter must have been miraculous.)

Mark the courage of Paul: "he got up and went back into the town" (v. 20b, TCNT).

(7) *Derbe* (14:20b, 21a). On the next day Paul and Barnabas made their way to Derbe, a city on the frontier of Galatia but not a great distance from Lystra. Luke makes no mention of anything special at Derbe. The reference to their making "many disciples," however, implies that their preaching met with great success at Derbe. Acts 20:4 speaks of a certain Gaius of Derbe who was a believer.

2. *The return to Antioch (14:21b-28)*. At Derbe Paul and his company were not very far from Tarsus, his home town, and to travel this way would have been the most direct route to Syrian Antioch. However, their concern for the congregations which had been formed in the course of their travels led them to retrace their steps, revisiting first the cities of Lystra, Iconium, and Pisidian Antioch (v. 21b). The object of the return trip was that of "confirming [strengthening,' RSV; 'reassuring,' TCNT; 'heartening,' NEB] the souls of the disciples, exhorting ['urging,' TCNT; 'encouraging,' Weymouth] them to continue in ['remain true to,' TCNT; 'hold fast to,' Weymouth] the faith," and reminding them "that through many tribulations we must enter into the kingdom of God" (v. 22, ASV). This does not mean that enduring sufferings merits entrance into the kingdom; the thought is that entering the kingdom is, in a world such as ours, necessarily attended by persecution and that we must be prepared to endure it.

As a further aid to the work, the apostles "appointed ['helped them select,' Williams] elders in every church" (v. 23a, ASV). In the months which separated the first and second visits there was time for the persons having gifts of leadership to become known. Having appointed the elders, the apostles engaged in a season of prayer and fasting with the entire membership and then "commended them to the Lord, on whom they had believed" (v. 23b, asv). "Commended" translates a word the idea of which is that of entrusting or depositing, as in a bank.

Leaving Antioch, the missionaries "passed through Pisidia and came to Pamphylia" (v. 24, asv), the region in which Perga was situated. It appears that on the outward journey they had only passed through Perga. Now, however, they spoke the word there. From Perga they proceeded to Attalia (the seaport of Perga), and from there they sailed directly to Antioch of Syria, "the place where they had been committed to the gracious care of God for the work which they had now finished" (vv. 24b-26, tcnt). Cyprus for some reason was not revisited on the return trip.

Thus the first journey came to an end. The apostles had preached the Gospel in the provinces of Cyprus, Pamphylia, and Galatia. At least four churches had been founded: in Pisidian Antioch, Iconium, Lystra, and Derbe. The space traversed, though considerable under the circumstances, was small compared with that covered by the second and third journeys.

It had been a long time (one to three years) since Paul and Barnabas had left Antioch, and the reunion must have been a joyful one. The apostles gathered the church together and "proceeded to report in detail all that God, working with them, had done" (v. 27a, Weymouth). They especially reported "how he had thrown open the gates of faith to the Gentiles" (v. 27b, neb). Carver comments that some years earlier (11:18), at Jerusalem, "it had been allowed that 'God gave to Gentiles repentance for life.' Now the missionaries declare that a door into the kingdom is opened for them, and it is a 'door of faith,' not of ceremonial or of racial accident" (p. 153). Luke gives no hint of the manner in which the report was received.

Following this, the apostles spent a considerable time with the disciples at Antioch (v. 28). Exactly how long they remained here, we are not told. Antioch, we may assume, was a favorite locale for Paul; "it gave him opportunities of work unsurpassed by any city except by Rome itself" (Lindsay, II, 60).

In summary, the following matters relative to the first journey should be noted: (1) the desertion of Mark, (2) the use of the name "Paul," (3) the ascendancy of Paul, (4) the recorded sermons of Paul, and (5) the missionary methods of the apostles. In reference to this three things emerge: (a) They chose the great centers of population, cities of influence, in which to plant the Gospel. (b) Their custom was to seek out a synagogue where possible and preach first to the Jews. These were the people who would have the best background for understanding the message of the Gospel. (c) They took great care to preserve the fruit of their work, by encouragement, instruction, and organization.

FOR FURTHER STUDY

1. Use a concordance to study all the references in Acts to the church at Antioch. What was there about this church which equipped it for launching the greatest missionary enterprise recorded in Acts?

2. Use a Bible dictionary to study Prophets and Teachers.

3. Use a map to trace the missionary journey of Barnabas and Saul. Why was Cyprus chosen as the first place to be visited?

CHAPTER 5

Jerusalem Conference

(Acts 15:1-35)

Chapter 14 closed with the statement that Paul and Barnabas "tarried no little time with the disciples" at Antioch (v. 28, ASV). (Hackett assigns this period to the years 48 and 49; more recent writers tend to favor an earlier date.) The opening words of chapter 15 suggest that it was during this extended stay of the apostles in Antioch that an unhappy contention arose between the Jewish and the Gentile converts. It was a contention of far-reaching significance and nearly had the effect of severing the Christian community into two hostile camps. The end result of the controversy was a journey by Paul and Barnabas to Jerusalem, where a solemn assembly of believers was called to resolve the problem. That meeting, often designated as "the Jerusalem conference" or "the Apostolic Council," is the story of Acts 15. The date was probably A.D. 48 or 49. (G. Ogg and Haenchen both date it A.D. 48; Hackett and Lindsay think the date to be A.D. 50.)

Traditionally the conference of Acts 15 has been identified with the Jerusalem visit recounted by Paul in Galatians 2:1-10 (cf. E. de W. Burton, *The Epistle to the Galatians* in "The International Critical Commentary"; H. N. Ridderbos, *The Epistle of Paul to the Churches of Galatia* in "The New International Commentary on the New Testament"; et al.). In recent years the view that the visit of Galatians 2:1-10 is identical with the famine visit of Acts 11:30 has attracted wide attention. Championed in modern times by Sir William Ramsay, this view is probably the prevailing view among British scholars today (cf. C. S. C. Williams, F. F. Bruce, et al.).[1] The present discussion follows the traditional interpretation.

---

[1]Some Continental scholars (e.g., Jeremias), followed by a number in Britain and America (e.g., K. Lake, A. D. Nock), look upon Acts 11:27-30 and Acts 15 as duplicate accounts of Galatians 2:1-10. Their contention is that these accounts reflect two sources which Luke failed to merge.

The passage under consideration may be divided as follows: (1) the occasion of the conference (vv. 1-3), (2) the deliberations of the conference (vv. 4-21), (3) the decision of the conference (vv. 22-29), and (4) the report to Antioch (vv. 30-35).

I. THE OCCASION OF THE CONFERENCE (vv. 1-3).

The occasion which made the conference necessary was the arrival in Antioch of "certain men" who "came down from Judaea and taught the brethren" that unless Gentiles committed themselves to the law of Moses by submitting to ritual circumcision they could not be saved (v. 1). Such teaching was contrary to the "door of faith" theology (cf. 14:27) to which Paul and Barnabas were committed and which up to this point had been consistently maintained in Antioch. The "certain men" who were promulgating this heresy were apparently representatives of the circumcision party in Jerusalem (cf. v. 5), a group to whom commentators often give the name "Judaizers."[2] It is implied in 15:24 that these men did not have the approval of the Jerusalem church in their mission to Antioch.

The issue must be clearly understood. Earlier (11:18) the church agreed that God had granted to the Gentiles the repentance which leads to life.[3] That is to say, the *possibility* of Gentile salvation was admitted. Now the question concerns the *grounds on which* or the means by which Gentiles may be saved.

The gravity of the matter was immediately recognized by Paul and Barnabas. They vigorously opposed the teachers from Jerusalem, and after fierce discussion and controversy it was decided that Paul and Barnabas, along with some other brethren from Antioch, should go to Jerusalem to confer with the apostles and elders about the issue (v. 2). In Galatians 2:2 Paul affirms that he went up to Jerusalem in obedience to a divine revelation. Precisely how this revelation came, he does not say, but it could have been given through the Holy Spirit to the church (cf. 13:1-3), and through the church to Paul and Barnabas. Galatians 2:1 informs us that Titus, a Gentile convert, was among those who accompanied Paul and Barnabas to Jerusalem.

Paul's intention in consulting with the Jerusalem apostles was not, we may be sure, to ascertain whether he and Barnabas were

---

[2]It is the teaching of the Judaizers which Paul combats and refutes in his epistle to the Galatians.

[3]Carver, however, feels that the church on that occasion was only conceding the conversion of Cornelius and his household *as an exceptional case*. It was not, according to Carver, the establishment of a general and abiding principle.

right or wrong in their proclamation of salvation for the Gentiles by the "door of faith." They were convinced of the rightness of the course which they were following, and as they made their way to Jerusalem they declared "the conversion of the Gentiles," that is, they related how non-Jews were turning to God for salvation. Their concern was rather to stop the mouths of the Judaizers, effect a proper understanding among the brethren, and work for the maintenance of unity in the church. The fear of the missionaries was that the opposition of the Jerusalem church — especially opposition of the leaders in that church — might render ineffectual both their past and future work among the Gentiles. Burton explains that Paul's "unshaken confidence in the divine origin and the truth of his own gospel did not prevent his seeing that the rupture which would result from a refusal of the pillar apostles . . . to recognize the legitimacy of his mission and gospel . . . would be disastrous alike to the Jewish and the Gentile parties which would thus be created" *(Galatians,* p. 73).

II. THE DELIBERATIONS OF THE CONFERENCE (vv. 4-21).

There were at least three meetings between the delegation from Antioch and the brethren at Jerusalem: (1) a public rception (vv. 4, 5), (2) a private meeting between Paul (and probably Barnabas) and the "pillars" of the Jerusalem church (cf. Gal. 2:3-10), and (3) the public conference at which a solemn decision was reached (vv. 6-21).

1. *The public reception (vv. 4, 5).* When the group arrived in Jerusalem "they were received of the church and the apostles and the elders" (v. 4a, ASV). This appears to have been a sort of public reception accorded the missionaries. At this meeting an account was given of their recently-concluded missionary journey. At the close of the meeting an emphatic protest was registered against the labors of Paul and Barnabas by the Pharisaic element within the church. Incensed that Gentiles had been taken into the church without first becoming Jewish proselytes, they vigorously insisted that "It is needful to circumcise them, and to charge them to keep the law of Moses" (v. 5, ASV).

2. *The public conference (vv. 7-21).* Luke does not tell of the private meeting between Paul and the three "pillar" apostles (cf. Gal. 2:3-10). The assembly referred to in verses 6ff. probably followed the private meeting, in which the four (perhaps five) leaders expressed complete confidence in one another and agreed in the action to be taken.

At the public meeting there were "the apostles" (i.e., the Jerusalem apostles, along with Barnabas and Paul[4] (v. 6), "elders" (i.e., elected office-bearers, v. 6), and "the multitude" (i.e., the congregation of believers, v. 12).

In the course of the conference there was (1) a speech by Peter (vv. 7-11), (2) a testimony by Barnabas and Paul (v. 12), and a speech by James (vv. 13-21).

Peter's speech (vv. 7-11) appears to have come after there had already been considerable discussion (v. 7a). Everyone was apparently given an opportunity to speak his mind. The apostle recalled his own experience in reference to the Cornelius episode, his point being that God had at that time clearly indicated that "he made no distinction" between Jews and Gentiles. To the latter he gave the Holy Spirit, "even as he did unto us" (vv. 7-9).

The apostle concluded that Jews and Gentiles are saved in the same manner — "through the grace of the Lord Jesus" (v. 11). Peter will not appear again in Acts.

The *testimony of Barnabas and Paul* (v. 12) was a rehearsing of the signs and wonders which God had wrought among the Gentiles through them. Observe the following: "Kept silence" is translated from the aorist tense, which might be rendered "became silent." The TCNT has "Every voice in the assembly was hushed." "Hearkened" (ASV), an imperfect tense, denotes a continuous hearing. The people "were listening to," giving rapt attention to, the missionaries. By pointing to the "signs and wonders" the missionaries were basing their case on facts, not words or argument.

The *speech of James* (vv. 13-21) was a summing up of the topic of discussion. Note the following: (1) This was James the half-brother to our Lord. James the brother of John had been executed earlier (12:1, 2). Many interpreters think that James was presiding over the meeting. (Carver, however, suggests that John, from whom no words are recorded in the chapter, had the responsibility of presiding.) (2) James insisted that the admission of Gentiles as reported by Peter was in complete agreement with the Old Testament. He quoted specifically Amos 9:1, 12 as Scripture proof that it had been God's purpose through the ages to call out the Gentiles (vv. 14-18). (3) James concluded that Jewish Christians should not impose unreasonable duties upon Gentile converts (v. 19); but the Gentiles, he explains, should be requested to respect their Jewish brethren's scruples, by avoiding such things as meat which had been offered to idols or from which the blood had not been drained and

---

[4]Notice that in Jerusalem, where Barnabas had been one of the most respected leaders of the church long before Paul's conversion, the order of the names reverts back to "Barnabas and Paul" (cf. v. 12).

by rejecting the low moral standards of the pagan world (v. 20). The Gentiles came out of an environment where even sin was sometimes regarded as religion. These suggestions of James were meant to help the new converts live a clean and moral life, as well as to make for better relations between Christians of Jewish and Gentile birth.

III. THE DECISION OF THE CONFERENCE (vv. 22-29).

What James expressed as his considered opinion commended itself to the Jerusalem leaders, and it became the deliverance of the entire assembly. It was then proposed (1) that certain chief men of the Jerusalem church be chosen to accompany Barnabas and Paul back to Antioch (v. 22) and (2) that a letter be sent along expressing the decision of the conference (vv. 23, 24).

The two men selected were "Judas Barsabbas," of whom nothing is known beyond what is said here, in 15:27, and in 15:32; and "Silas," who (like Judas Barsabbas) was a prophet (cf. 15:32). Silas, who later was selected by Paul to accompany him on his second missionary journey, is mentioned frequently in chapters 15 through 18 of Acts, in the salutations of three epistles of Paul, and once in 1 Peter (5:12). In the epistles the name always is given as "Silvanus," which probably was the Roman equivalent of the Hebrew "Silas."

The epistle, which Lindsay calls "the Magna Charta of Gentile Christianity," recounts the occasion of the trouble, suggesting that the disturbers had not had the approval of the Jerusalem church (vv. 23, 24). Next, the letter asserts the church's love for and confidence in Barnabas and Paul, thus vindicating their ministry (vv. 25, 26). Finally, the decision of the conference is stated (vv. 27-29).

In verse 28 two things are worthy of observation: (1) The letter claims that the church had the guidance of the Holy Spirit in reaching its decision. (2) The "necessary things" were things necessary for the maintenance of fellowship between Jewish and Gentile Christians, not for salvation.

IV. THE REPORT TO ANTIOCH (vv. 30-35).

The two chosen men (Judas Barsabbas and Silas), together with Paul and Barnabas, left immediately for Antioch. The believers of Antioch, having been called together, heard the epistle read; the effect was both joy and encouragement (vv. 30, 31). Judas and Silas, being themselves prophets, further encouraged and strengthened the brethren (v. 32).

When the time came for Judas and Silas to return to Jerusalem,

Paul and Barnabas remained in Antioch, teaching and preaching the word together with other colleagues in ministry (vv. 33, 35).[5]

The importance of the Jerusalem council is seen at three points: First, it decisively confirmed the principle of salvation by grace. Second, by affirming the Christian's freedom from Jewish legalism it showed that Christianity by its very nature transcends racial, national, social, and cultural bounds. Third, it demonstrated a practical method of settling church problems, namely by democratic procedure under the guidance of the Holy Spirit.

FOR FURTHER STUDY

1. Use a Bible dictionary to study the Judaizers.
2. Compare Acts 15 and Galatians 2:1-10.
3. Read an article on Silas in a Bible dictionary.

---

[5]Verse 34 of KJV, which states that Silas remained in Antioch, is not in the best Greek text and is accordingly omitted from ASV, RSV, etc.

CHAPTER 6

Witness in Macedonia and Achaia

(The Second Missionary Journey of Paul)
(Acts 15:36—18:22)

The settlement of the question of Gentile salvation (Acts 15:1-35) prepared the way for a great leap forward in the missionary enterprise. The second missionary journey, which Luke now records, takes the Gospel from the Oriental to the Hellenic world, from the Eastern Mediterranean cities of Jerusalem and Antioch to the Greek cities of Philippi, Thessalonica, Athens, and Corinth.

This journey, much more extensive than the first, spanned a period of three or four years (A.D. 49-52; Ogg, A.D. 48-51). The original purpose of the apostles in projecting this journey was to visit the churches previously established, to see how they were faring (15:36). God, however, had other and larger plans. Paul's companions on the journey were Silas (who was with him from the beginning), Timothy (who joined him at Lystra), and Luke (who joined him at Troas). Silas took the place of Barnabas, Timothy the place of Mark. Luke was perhaps Paul's personal physician.

Although other areas were visited, this journey centered mainly in Macedonia and Achaia. In Luke's account mention is made of (1) the contention between Paul and Barnabas (15:36-40), (2) the work in Syro-Cilicia (15:41), (3) at Lystra and Derbe (16:1-5), (4) in Troas (16:6-10), (5) in Philippi (16:11-40), (6) in Thessalonica (17:1-9), (7) in Berea (17:10-14), (8) in Athens (17:15-34), (9) in Corinth (18:1-17), and (10) the return to Antioch (18:18-22).

I. THE CONTENTION BETWEEN PAUL AND BARNABAS (15:36-40).

It was Paul who proposed to Barnabas that they return to the places where they had preached on their first journey (v. 36). Barnabas apparently shared Paul's concern for the young converts and suggested that they take with them John Mark (v. 37). But

Paul, remembering that Mark had deserted the missionary company in the midst of the first journey, did not think this was a good idea (v. 38). This difference of opinion resulted in a "sharp contention" (NIV, "sharp disagreement") — so sharp, in fact, that Barnabas and Paul parted (v. 39).

It is not possible to know who was right in this matter. Carver thinks Barnabas was right in wanting and being willing to give Mark a second chance; Paul was right, he says, in hesitating to trust a deserter. Knowling explains that the outcome was good, "for Mark was stirred up to greater diligence by Paul, and the kindness of Barnabas made him cling to him all the more devotedly" (p. 331). Barclay adds that "it may well have been the friendship of Barnabas, the man of the kindly heart, which gave Mark back his self-respect and which made him determined to make good. The greatest thing a man can have is someone who believes in him" (p. 128).

Later, Mark proved himself, and Paul wrote to Timothy from prison requesting that he bring Mark with him, "for he is profitable unto me" (2 Tim. 4:11).

In the providence of God there were now two missionary parties. Barnabas and Mark went to Cyprus, the native land of the older man (v. 39b); Paul chose Silas (v. 40), and the two of them traveled by land to the area of Asia Minor. It appears from Acts 16:37f. that Silas, like Paul, was a Roman citizen. Neither Barnabas nor Mark is mentioned again in Acts.

II. THE WORK IN SYRO-CILICIA (15:41).

The work in Syro-Cilicia is mentioned only in summary fashion. The district of Syria which was visited was likely that north of Antioch. Cilicia, it will be remembered, was the home province of Paul. The churches in Syria were probably established as a result of work done by Paul (and others, perhaps) out of Antioch. Those in Cilicia must have been founded by him during that period between his forced departure from Jerusalem (9:30) and his enlistment by Barnabas for work in Antioch (11:25, 26). Indeed, the churches in both Cilicia and Syria might have been the result of Paul's labors during this period of his life.

III. THE WORK AT DERBE AND LYSTRA (16:1-5).

At Derbe and Lystra there were churches established by Paul and Barnabas on their first journey. Three things of note are mentioned in the present passage: (1) the enlistment of Timothy for the missionary party (vv. 1-3), (2) the delivering of the decrees which resulted from the Jerusalem conference (vv. 4, 5), and (3) the growth of the churches (v. 5).

In reference to Timothy mention is made of his family (cf. 2 Tim. 1:5), with attention being called to the fact that his father was a Gentile (v. 1); his good reputation (v. 2); and his submitting to the rite of circumcision (v. 3). It would appear that Paul had Timothy circumcised out of deference to Jewish prejudice, since Timothy was part Jew. Without this, Timothy would not have been permitted to preach in the synagogues. It was "a question of efficient service, not an essential of salvation" (Robertson, 244). It is reasonable to suppose that Timothy's conversion occurred under the ministry of Paul and Barnabas on the first journey. In 1 Corinthians 4:17 Paul calls him "my ... child in the Lord." Robertson estimates his age at the time he joined Paul to have been about eighteen years (p. 243).

Timothy's name occurs no fewer than seventeen times in ten different epistles of Paul, more than any other companion of Paul. And two of Paul's thirteen extant letters were addressed to him. Horton writes that "we have no words from his lips, no letters from his pen. . . . Paul loved him; that is all. . . . Timothy comes before us for fourteen or at most eighteen years, and vanishes, never to be forgotten, never to be known, loved not for his own sake, but because Paul loved him" *(Pastoral Epistles)*.

The decrees (vv. 3, 4) were probably especially meaningful when delivered by Silas, one of the two leaders of the Jerusalem church chosen to take to Antioch the apostolic letter which contained those decrees. We may imagine that a copy of the decrees was left with each church.

The growth of the churches (v. 5) was both spiritual and numerical. This is the fourth such summary in Acts of the growth of the work (cf. 6:7; 9:31; 12:24).

IV. THE WORK AT TROAS (16:6-10).

For a time Paul must have been perplexed about the direction his work should take. The doors all seemed to be closing. He and his companions passed first through "the region of Phrygia and Galatia" (ASV),[1] the region in which Pisidian Antioch and Iconium

---

[1]This rendering is preferable to "Phrygia and the region of Galatia" (KJV). The article, which occurs only before "Phrygia," brackets the two names together as modifiers of "region." The region was so called because it was often designated "Galatic Phrygia." Ramsay calls it "the Phrygian region of *the province* of Galatia" *(St. Paul the Traveller,* p. 194; cf. TCNT). Bruce understands "Galatia" here to be used in its popular rather than its political (provincial) sense and says the phrase denotes the boundary between the ethnic regions of Phrygia and Galatia.

were located. The populous province of Asia, with cities such as Ephesus, Laodicea, and Hierapolis, lay just ahead; and to this district Paul wanted to go. But in some undefined way he and his companions had been "forbidden[2] of the Holy Spirit to speak the word in Asia" (v. 6, ASV). How the Spirit communicated His will in this matter we are not told. It may have been by inner prompting or by the overruling of external circumstances. Barclay, calling attention to the sudden emergence of Luke on the scene (v. 10), suggests that it may have been ill health which barred the apostle. Bruce conjectures that the Spirit spoke through a prophet in the church at Lystra.

Having failed to receive divine approval for preaching the Gospel in Asia,[3] the missionaries traveled north from Pisidian Antioch until "they were come over against Mysia" (v. 7, ASV). Bruce takes this to mean "something like 'opposite the eastern border of Mysia' (the northwestern region of the province of Asia)" (p. 326). Rieu renders it, "When they came to a point east of Mysia."

The intention of Paul and his companions was to continue northward and enter Bithynia, a territory which in 74 B.C. had been bequeathed to Rome by its last king. In New Testament times Bithynia and Pontus were administered as a single Roman province. Again, the plans of the missionaries were divinely forbidden; "the Spirit of Jesus[4] suffered them not" to enter (v. 7b, ASV). They then "skirted Mysia and reached the coast at Troas" (v. 8, NEB). This city, founded by Alexander the Great near the site of the old city of Troy, was the main port for vessels traveling between Asia and Macedonia.

At Troas, two significant things occurred. First, the negative leading of the Spirit gave place to positive. In a night vision Paul saw "a man of Macedonia, beseeching him, and saying, Come over into Macedonia, and help us" (v. 9, ASV; Williams, "a man from Macedonia kept standing and pleading with him . . ."). This provided the guidance which the missionaries had been seeking, and so immediately they "set about getting a passage to Macedonia" (v.

---

[2]An aorist participle is used in the Greek, suggesting that the prohibition was received before they left Lystra.

[3]The prohibition concerned *preaching* the word in Asia, not *traveling* through Asia. It was necessary for them to pass through a part of Asia in order to reach either Bithynia or Troas.

[4]Observe this unusual way of designating the Spirit. "The Holy Spirit is the Spirit of Jesus and His coming fulfills Christ's promise when He said, *Lo, I am with you always, even unto the end of the world*" (Lindsay, II, 72). Bruner remarks that "the Spirit is not to be dissociated from Jesus. The Spirit *is* Jesus at work in continuation of his ministry" (p. 156).

10, NEB), concluding that God had summoned them to preach the Gospel there.

Second, Luke joined the missionary party. This is reflected by the sudden change from the use of third person pronouns ("he," "they," "them," etc.) to the use of the first person plural ("we," "us"). The reader can from this point, by noticing the "we" sections of Acts (16:10-17; 20:5-15; 21:1-18; 27:1—28:16),[5] determine when Luke is writing as an eyewitness of the events narrated.

V. THE WORK AT PHILIPPI (16:11-40).

Setting sail from Troas, the missionaries "made a straight course [Williams, 'struck a bee line'] to Samothrace" and reached that small Aegean island at the end of the first day. On the following day they arrived at "Neapolis" ("New Town"), which lay about ten miles southeast of Philippi and served as its seaport (v. 11, ASV). Paul and his party disembarked at Neapolis (modern Kavalla) and made their way to Philippi.

Gateway between Asia and the West, Philippi was "a city of [the Roman province] of Macedonia" (v. 12a). In an earlier period it was called Crenides, but in the fourth century B.C. Philip II of Macedon (Alexander's father) enlarged and fortified the city and renamed it for himself. In 168 B.C. Macedonia fell into the hands of the Romans, and little is known about the fortunes of Philippi for a hundred years. In 42 B.C. Octavius (Augustus) and Mark Antony defeated Cassius and Brutus in the valley where Philippi was located. This victory marked the downfall of the Republic and the beginning of the Roman Empire. It was shortly after this that Augustus, as a memorial of his victory, made Philippi a Roman colony. That is to say, he peopled it with Roman soldiers, endowed it with special privileges, and made it a military outpost. At present, Philippi is a scene of ruins.

Luke describes Philippi as "a city of Macedonia, the first of the district"[6] (v. 12a, ASV; KJV, "the chief city of that part of Macedonia"). This expression has given rise to considerable discussion, since it is generally recognized that in Paul's day Thessalonica was capital of the province of Macedonia and Amphipolis, not Philippi, was the chief city of this administrative district. Coneybeare and Howson understand the phrase to mean that Philippi was the first

---

[5]Guthrie feels that there "is no need . . . to limit the we-section too narrowly to those passages where the first person actually occurs" (*Introduction*, p. 334).
[6]Macedonia was divided by the Romans into four administrative districts, but Vincent (*Philippians*) says this was 200 years before Paul and that the arrangement lasted only twenty-two years.

Macedonian city to be reached by Paul, omitting Neapolis because it was only the seaport (p. 250). Hackett, on the basis of the absence of the Greek article, renders it "a chief city of the province of Macedonia" (p. 184). Ramsay thinks Luke was a native of Philippi and that his pride in his own city led him to describe it as a city of chief importance in its part of Macedonia (cf. NEB). Vincent thinks the meaning may be that Philippi was the most considerable colonial city in its part of Macedonia. Robertson thinks that though Philippi was neither the capital nor the largest city of its district it may have ranked as most important because of its strategic position. Bruce thinks the meaning may be simply "a city of the first district of Macedonia" (p. 330). Munck says "chief city" was an honorary title given to important cities (p. 161).

Four significant occurrences in Philippi are recorded:

1. *The conversion of Lydia and her household (vv. 13-15).* The "man of Macedonia" turned out to be a woman (!) who was a god-fearer (v. 14). She was from Thyatira, a city in the province of Asia, where the missionaries had earlier been forbidden of the Spirit to speak the word. The city was famous for its purple dyes. Some think Lydia was a seller of purple cloth (cf. TCNT), others that she sold purple dye (cf. Rieu). Her conversion was, in contrast to Paul's (ch. 9), quiet and unspectacular. The Lord simply opened her heart as she listened to the Gospel (v. 14b). The impression left by the text is that she was perhaps a widow. Her "household," who also became Christians (v. 15), would include servants and other dependents. Practical proof of Lydia's conversion was given when she extended the hospitality of her home to the missionaries (v. 15b).

2. *The deliverance of a demon-possessed girl (vv. 16-18).* A slave girl who is described as "having a spirit of divination" (v. 16, ASV) met and followed Paul and his companions as they were going to the place of prayer. "Spirit of divination" (lit., "a spirit, a python") characterizes her as a person inspired by Apollo, the god worshiped at Pytho (Delphi) in central Greece. Plutarch used the word *python* for a ventriloquist soothsayer. In the Septuagint it is used of those who had a "familiar spirit" (cf. the witch of Endor).

For many days this girl annoyed the missionaries (vv. 17, 18a). Then Paul, unable to endure it any longer, turned and charged the evil spirit within her to come out. "And it came out that very hour" (v. 18c, ASV).

3. *The conversion of the jailor (vv. 9-34).* The event which led the way to the jailor's conversion was the arrest and imprisonment

of Paul and Silas (vv. 19-24). The real cause of their arrest is stated in verse 19; the trumped-up charge is stated in verses 20 and 21. Their accusers paraded their patriotism, but it was their love of money which really motivated them. Luke calls attention to the cruelty of the treatment given the missionaries (vv. 22-24), their uncommon reaction to this (v. 25), and God's response to their prayers (v. 26).

The terror, conviction, and conversion of the jailor are reported in detail (vv. 27-34). Roused from his sleep by the earthquake and seeing that the prison doors were open, the jailor concluded that the prisoners had escaped. Having a Roman soldier's sense of duty and discipline, he drew his short sword and was about to thrust it through his heart or throat when Paul called aloud to assure him that not any of the prisoners had fled. Thereupon the jailor called for a light and rushed into the presence of the preachers.

The jailor's question, "Sirs, what must I do to be saved?," was prompted by an accumulation of things: the unusual character and conduct of Paul and Silas, the strange occurrences of the night, and so on. He had perhaps heard the slave girl's cry that these men were proclaiming "a way of salvation" (cf. v. 17). "He may thus far have understood little of what it was to be saved, but he had a conscience and in the presence of good men and God he stood condemned" (Carver, p. 171). Paul and Silas, in response to the soldier's question, explained how believing in the Lord Jesus would save him, and also his household (v. 31). The Gospel was preached to "all that were in his house" (v. 32), and in that very night the jailor "washed their stripes" and he and all his house were baptized, "immediately" (vv. 33, 34). The washing of the stripes of the missionaries and the extending of the hospitality of his home were indications of the complete change which had come over the jailor.

4. *The release of Paul and Silas (vv. 35-40).* When it was morning, the magistrates of Philippi, "sent the police, saying 'Let those men go'" (v. 35, RSV). What led them to this decision we are not told. Perhaps they had a deepening conviction that the missionaries had been unjustly treated. The news of the earthquake may have had something to do with it.

When told of this by the jailor, Paul replied in pointed fashion. He declared that it was in violation of Roman law that they had been beaten — in the most shameful manner ("publicly") and without a trial ("uncondemned") (v. 37). The magistrates were distressed when they learned that the preachers were Roman citizens and, perhaps fearful of more trouble, came personally to the prison to request that they leave the city (vv. 38, 39). After calling at the house of Lydia, visiting the brethren, and comforting them, Paul and his company left Philippi.

It is reasonable to suppose that Luke remained in Philippi (note "they," v. 40).

VI. The Work in Thessalonica (17:1-9).

Leaving Philippi, Paul and his companions traveled westward through "Amphipolis" (thirty miles from Philippi) and "Apollonia" (thirty miles from Amphipolis) and "came to Thessalonica."

A little more than a hundred miles from Philippi, Thessalonica (modern Salonika) was an important commercial center and the most populous city (200,000 people) of Macedonia. It was founded in 315 B.C. by Cassander, king of Macedonia, and named for his wife, who was the half sister of Alexander the Great. When the Romans conquered Macedonia in 168 B.C. they divided the country into four districts and made Thessalonica the capital of its district. In 146 B.C., when the four districts were merged into a single province, Thessalonica became virtually the capital of the whole. Some time later it was made a free city, which meant that its people had self-government of a sort. The administration of the city was in the hands of a board of five or six magistrates known as politarchs.

Paul's ministry in the city, described in verses 2-4, took him to the synagogue, where on three successive sabbaths he reasoned[7] with the worshipers. A threefold argument was used: He showed from the Scriptures (1) that the Messiah therein promised was to be a suffering Messiah, (2) that He was to rise from the dead, and (3) that Jesus of Nazareth is the fulfillment of these prophecies. (See 1 Thess. 1 and 2 for a fuller account of Paul's work in Thessalonica.)

Opposition to Paul's work is described in verses 5-9. It was led by Jews who, moved by jealousy, enlisted the aid of "certain vile fellows of the rabble" (v. 5, ASV; NEB, "low fellows from the dregs of the populace"; Norlie: "wicked rowdies"). Getting a crowd together, they threw the city into an uproar and attacked the house of Jason, where the missionaries had been staying. Angered because they could not find the missionaries, they dragged Jason and some of the brethren before the rulers of the city, crying, "These men who have caused trouble all over the world have now come here, and Jason has welcomed them into his house. They are

---

[7]The Greek word originally meant "to converse," but "it came to denote *discussion* by means of question and answer.... Here ... the word is used in the more general sense of reasoning or arguing" (Rackham, pp. 294-295). Souter defines it "I address, preach, lecture."

all defying Caesar's decrees, saying that there is another king, one called Jesus" (vv. 6, 7, NIV). These words alarmed the crowd, and also the magistrates; but their action was cautious. Jason and the others were made to post bond (perhaps as a guarantee that the missionaries would leave the city and not return) and then they were released (v. 9). The Thessalonian correspondence (1 Thess. 2:14; 3:1-5; 2 Thess. 1:6) indicates that the believers of Thessalonica were severely persecuted after Paul's departure from the city.

VII. THE WORK IN BEREA (17:10-14).

The brethren of Thessalonica sent Paul and Silas away by night to Berea (modern Verria), about fifty miles west of Thessalonica. In his account of their work there, Luke calls attention to the noble character of the Bereans (v. 11a; Knox, "a better breed than" the Thessalonians), their readiness to receive the word (v. 11b), the success of the work (v. 12), the opposition which was stirred up by Jews who came down from Thessalonica (v. 13), and the speedy departure of Paul from Berea (v. 14). Compare verses 10 and 14, noting the mention of Timothy in the latter verse. He apparently joined Paul and Silas after they had reached Berea.

Some of the Berean brethren escorted Paul as far as Athens. Luke had been left behind in Thessalonica; Silas and Timothy remained in Berea (v. 15). Paul, therefore, was for some time alone in the city.

VIII. THE WORK IN ATHENS (17:15-34).

Situated in the Roman province of Achaia, Athens was the most illustrious city of ancient Greece. Celebrated as the home of classical literature and art and famous for its political and intellectual achievements, it had every reason to be proud of its history. By New Testament times the glory of the city had long been in eclipse, but it was still the intellectual center of the Roman world.

In telling the story of Paul's work in Athens, Luke focuses attention on four matters: (1) the preacher (v. 16), (2) the audience (vv. 17-21), (3) the message (vv. 22-31), and (4) the response (vv. 32-34).

1. *The preacher (v. 16).* The brethren who escorted Paul to Athens had been sent back to Berea with instructions for Silas and Timothy to rejoin the apostle in Athens as soon as possible. While he waited for them, "his spirit was stirred in him, when he saw the city wholly given to idolatry" (v. 16). "Was stirred" comes from the Greek word from which "paroxysm" comes. The modern tourist may look upon the remains of Athenian architecture and sculpture

and admire them as works of art, but to Paul they were temples and images of pagan deities, and his response was one of indignation, grief, and compassion. Convinced as he was of the truth of Christianity, the apostle saw this elaborate display of idolatrous worship as an insult to the majesty of God.

2. *The audience (vv. 17-21).* Paul's reaction was not simply one of feeling; he was stirred to action by what he saw. A city so wholly dedicated to false religion, he felt, must be given the Gospel. "Therefore disputed he in the synagogue with the Jews, and with the devout persons, and in the market daily with them that met with him" (v. 17).

"Devout persons" was used of Gentiles who failed to find satisfaction in their pagan worship and embraced the ethical monotheism of the Jews. They attended the Jewish synagogues but did not obligate themselves to keep the Mosaic law. They are to be distinguished from proselytes, who submitted to circumcision and yielded to the full demands of the Mosaic law.

"The market" was an open space, usually in the heart of the city, where business, both judicial and commercial, was transacted. Around it were grouped the public buildings of the city (temples, law courts, etc.), colonnades (used as places of concourse), and an abundance of shops. The marketplace was the chief place of concourse for an ancient city and the focus of its civic life. The Athenian marketplace doubtless had all the usual adjuncts and was the place where philosophers lectured to their pupils.

The "Epicureans" were followers of Epicurus, an Athenian philosopher (341-270 B.C.) who held, among other things, that pleasure was the chief end of life. Epicureanism has been described as a philosophy of materialism and despair; it accepted the existence of gods but taught that they took no interest in human affairs. The "Stoics" claimed as their founder Zeno, a native of Cyprus who moved to Athens and flourished around 300 B.C. The name of his school was derived from the fact that he taught in a painted *stoa* (portico). The Stoics taught that men should live in harmony with reason. In theology they were pantheistic. At its best the system was marked by great moral earnestness, but it was strongly tinged with fatalism and often fostered a spiritual pride utterly foreign to the teachings of Christianity.

Paul's encounter in the marketplace resulted in his being brought before "the Areopagus" (v. 19). The word means "hill of Ares," Ares being the Greek name of the war god whom the Romans called Mars. Areopagus was both the name of a place (located northwest of the Acropolis in Athens and crowned with a temple erected to Mars) and of an aristocratic council or court of Athenians. This court, called Areopagus because at an earlier time it held its sessions on the famous hill, was the most august body in Athens and commanded great respect of the people. The reference here and in verse 22 is likely to the court of the Areopagus. Paul was brought before this court, not so much to be tried in a judicial sense, but, as a strange lecturer, to give an account of his teaching.

3. *The message (vv. 22-31).* Paul's explanation took the form of a sermon about God (vv. 22-31). In it he emphasized these things: (1) The Deity is a personal, living God who made the world and everything in it; and because He is sovereign Lord of all, He cannot be contained in human shrines (v. 24). (2) He is a God of might and majesty who, far from being dependent on His creatures, gives to them "life, and breath, and all things" (v. 25). (3) He made "from one" all nations of men. He guides and governs in human history, and He is within the reach of all if they will only seek Him (vv. 26-29). (4) One day God will judge all men through Jesus Christ, and because this is so He now commands all men to repent (vv. 30, 31).

4. *The response (vv. 32-34).* Some of the hearers "mocked" or ridiculed what Paul preached — the idea of a resurrection of dead men was to them absurd. Others politely suggested that they might "hear" more of the apostle's teaching at a later time. Whether this indicated a serious intention or was simply a courteous dismissal, we cannot know. But over against these two groups was another (v. 34) who attached themselves to the apostle and believed. Among these was Dionysius, a member of the court of Areopagus, and a woman named Damaris.

IX. THE WORK IN CORINTH (18:1-17).

One of the most important cities of ancient Greece, Corinth was located fifty miles west of Athens on a narrow isthmus overlooking the Adriatic and Aegean Seas (more precisely, the Gulf of Corinth and the Saronic Gulf). This isthmus connects the Peloponnesus (southern Greece) with mainland Greece.

Corinth was founded in ancient times, and by 750 B.C. it was the wealthiest city in Greece. In 146 B.C. the Romans, under Mummius, destroyed the ancient city. Its citizens were killed or sold into slavery. Its buildings were wrecked, its art treasures taken to Rome, and rebuilding was forbidden. For a hundred years the city lay in ruins; then in 46 B.C. Julius Caesar rebuilt Corinth and colonized it with veterans and freedmen. The new Corinth soon became the capital of the province of Achaia and regained the place of prominence which it had known in ancient times.

If the two seaports of Corinth (Lechaeum on the west and Cenchraea on the east) are included, the population of Corinth was perhaps as great as 600,000. One writer says there were 200,-000 freedmen and half a million slaves.

Corinth was generally considered the foulest city of the ancient world. So notorious was it for drunkenness, debauchery, and dishonesty that "to live like a Corinthian" *(corinthiazomai)* became a popular saying for living a loose life. Liddell and Scott give "to practice whoredom" as its definition. "Corinthian girl" was synonymous with prostitute. An inscription found in the amphitheater implies that there were reserved seats for prostitutes. Romans 1:18ff., written while Paul was in Corinth on a subsequent visit, probably reflects the quality of life which the apostle witnessed there.

Even the religion of Corinth was permeated with gross immorality. At the temple of Aphrodite, located on top of the Acrocorinthus, a thousand young women served as priestesses. In reality they were religious prostitutes, living daily in impurity and indulging in lascivious dances at the public festivals. At night they walked the streets to seduce the men whom they met. Moffatt explains that though the temple was not rebuilt after its destruction in 146 B.C., the religion of Aphrodite thrived in the various shrines about the city and about the docks.

Luke's account of Paul's ministry in Corinth centers about (1) the meeting with Aquila and Priscilla (vv. 1-3), (2) the campaign in the city (vv. 4-11), and (3) Paul's experience before Gallio (vv. 12-17).

"Aquila and Priscilla" were Jews who had recently come to Corinth from Rome. Luke explains that their departure from Rome came as a result of Claudius' (emperor from A.D. 41-54) edict, issued in A.D. 49, expelling Jews from the city. In Romans 16:3 we learn that Aquila and Priscilla later returned to Rome. Aquila, like Paul, was a tentmaker.

The campaign in the city began in the synagogue (v. 4). Because he was working as a tentmaker, most of Paul's preaching probably had to be done on the sabbath. But with the arrival of Silas and Timothy, who seem to have brought an offering (cf. 2 Cor. 11:9), Paul was enabled to give his whole time to preaching (v. 5, NIV). The offering likely came from the Philippian church, which had earlier helped the apostle while he was in Thessalonica (cf. Phil. 4:14-16).

Because of opposition from the Jews Paul was forced to take his work to the home of Titus Justus (v. 7), a God-fearer whose house was next door to the synagogue. An indication of the success of Paul's ministry in Corinth is found in the reference to "Crispus, the ruler of the synagogue, [who] believed in the Lord with all his house" (v. 8a, ASV). In addition, many other Corinthians also became believers and were baptized (v. 8b).

Encouragement was given the apostle by a night vision (vv. 9, 10). In it the Lord (1) told him not to be afraid but to speak boldly, (2) assured him of His protecting care, and (3) in effect promised him an abundant harvest for his labors. That such a vision was given may indicate that the apostle had become discouraged, perhaps because of the fierce opposition he was encountering from the Jews, the gross immorality of the city, and sheer loneliness.

After the vision Paul remained in Corinth a year and a half. The full length of his stay in the city may have been about two years.

The experience with Gallio is important for fixing the date of Paul's visit to Corinth, and for determining the general chronology of his life. Gallio, a son of the elder Seneca (50 B.C.-A.D. 40) and brother of the younger Seneca (3 B.C.-A.D. 65), was proconsul of Achaia for about two and a half years. From an inscription found at Delphi about the turn of the century, it can be inferred that his proconsulship began in July, A.D. 51 (cf. Bruce, pp. 373, 374; Haenchen says "about the first of May 51," p. 67). It may be assumed that when the encounter with Gallio occurred Paul had been in Corinth for perhaps a year (cf. vv. 11, 18). Bruce thinks Paul appeared before the proconsul shortly after the latter's arrival in Corinth, and that he tarried in Corinth for several months after the episode (p. 377). Haenchen dates the arrival of Paul in Corinth in the winter of A.D. 49/50; Ogg *(New Bible Dictionary)* and Hiebert *(Zondervan Pictorial Bible Dictionary)* put it in 50.

The charge brought against Paul was that of preaching an illegal religion (v. 13). Gallio, however, decided that the dispute was one which was strictly Jewish, that what Paul was propagating was simply a variety of Judaism. He had no intention of getting involved in that (vv. 14, 15), and accordingly had Paul's accusers ejected from the court (v. 16). The bystanders — probably Gentiles — seized on this as an occasion for venting their anti-Jewish feelings. Turning on Sosthenes, ruler of the synagogue, they beat him in front of the court. "But Gallio showed no concern whatever" (v. 17, NIV).

121

X. The Return to Antioch (18:18-22).

Paul stayed in Corinth for some time after his appearance before Gallio, then left for Syria, accompanied as far as Ephesus by Priscilla and Aquila. Before leaving Cenchrea (seaport for Corinth), however, he had his hair cut off because he had taken a vow (v. 18). We may assume that it was a vow connected in some way with his work in Corinth.

Leaving Ephesus the apostle sailed to Caesarea, the port for Palestine. Having landed at Caesarea, "he went up [probably to Jerusalem] and greeted the church and then went down to Antioch" in Syria (v. 22, NIV).

For Further Study

1. Make a list of Paul's companions on his second missionary journey.

2. Use a map to trace the course of this second journey.

3. List the different references to the leadership of the Spirit in the story of the second missionary journey.

4. How significant was the decision to preach in Macedonia? Explain.

CHAPTER 7

Witness in Ephesus and Asia

(The Third Missionary Journey of Paul)
(Acts 18:23—21:16)

Paul's residence at Antioch, in the interval between the second and third journeys, seems not to have been lengthy (cf. Knowling, p. 396). Bruce thinks the succession of participles in verses 22 and 23 gives an impression of haste. Smith thinks he spent the winter of A.D. 51/52 there, and in the spring of A.D. 52 set out on his third journey. Haenchen prefers the summer of 52 as the departure date; Ogg, 53; Hiebert, 54. The journey lasted about four or perhaps five years, with the work concentrated mainly in Ephesus and the province of Asia.

It appears that Paul began this journey alone. Various companions in travel are mentioned, however, in the course of the journey. Indeed, the names of seven who accompanied him from Macedonia into Asia are given (cf. 19:22, 29; 20:4).

I. THE TRIP THROUGH THE GALATIAN COUNTRY AND PHRYGIA (18:23).

The third journey, like the second, began as a journey of visitation to churches which had been previously established. Setting out from Antioch, the apostle traveled from place to place throughout the Galatic region (i.e., "Galatic Lycaonia," which, says Bruce, lay not in the province of Galatia, but in the territory of King Antiochus," p. 380) and Phrygia, which Bruce thinks included both Galatic and Asian Phrygia. The ministry in this area was that of strengthening and encouraging the believers.

II. THE MEETING OF APOLLOS WITH AQUILLA AND PRISCILLA (18:24-28).

This episode seems to be brought into the narrative to prepare the reader for Paul's finding the twelve disciples of John the Baptist in Ephesus (19:1ff.), though it is not said that they were in any way associated with Apollos. Apollos[1] is described as a native of Alexandria, a strategic city of North Africa which had a large Jewish community. Founded by and named for Alexander the Great in 332 B.C., Alexandria replaced Memphis as the seat of government in Egypt and was the center of Hellenistic culture for three centuries or more. In New Testament times it was the second largest city in the Empire, surpassed only by Rome. Blaiklock, who estimates its population to have been as great as a million, says it was more like a modern metropolis than any other ancient city (*Cities of the New Testament*). In its multi-racial character, he likens it to Singapore; in its array of public buildings, parks, and gardens, to Washington, D.C.

Apollos had been "instructed in the way of the Lord" and spoke and taught accurately "the story of Jesus" (Rieu),[2] although he knew "only the baptism of John" (v. 25). We are not told how or where he received his instruction; for all we know, it could have been in Alexandria. The baptism of John "differed from that of the apostles mainly in these respects: first, that theirs recognized a Messiah who had come; and secondly, that it was attested by the extraordinary gifts of the Spirit (19:6)" (Hackett, p. 218).

Other things told us about Apollos emphasize his rich endowment for ministry: an "eloquent [NIV, 'learned'] man" (v. 24), "mighty [RSV, 'well versed'] in the scriptures" (v. 24; Rieu, "a great authority on the scriptures"; Goodspeed, "skilful in the use of . . ."); "fervent in spirit" (v. 25, ASV; TCNT, "with burning zeal"; Goodspeed, "glowing with the Spirit"); gifted as a teacher (note "spake and taught accurately," v. 25, ASV); bold in preaching (v. 26a).

Impressed with Apollos' remarkable qualities and potential for ministry, but sensing some deficiencies in his understanding of the Gospel, Aquila and Priscilla invited him to their home "and expounded the new way to him in greater detail" (v. 26, NEB).

Some time later Apollos crossed over to Corinth (cf. 18:27; 19:1), carrying with him a letter of recommendation to the Corin-

---

[1]Carter and Earle, commenting on the strangeness of a man designated as a Jew bearing the name of a pagan god, cite Clarke's suggestion that Apollos' parents were Gentiles who were converted to Judaism after the birth of Apollos. Thus he was, on this theory, "A Jew by religion but not by nationality" (p. 275).

[2]The things that Apollos taught at this time probably were these: (1) that John was the forerunner of the Messiah, (2) that he had pointed out the Messiah as the Lamb of God who takes away the sin of the world, and (3) that this Messiah was Jesus of Nazareth.

thian church from his Ephesian friends (cf. 2 Cor. 3:1-3). His ministry in Corinth, sketched in a single sentence by Luke (18:27b, 28), was attended by divine favor and power. Paul, in 1 Corinthians 3:6, speaks of Apollos as watering the seed which he had planted. Other indications in 1 Corinthians show that there was no rivalry between the two men (cf. 1 Cor. 4:9; 16:12).

III. The Work in Ephesus (19:1-41).

While Apollos was at Corinth, Paul passed through "the upper country" (19:1, asv; tcnt, "the inland districts of Roman Asia"; Montgomery, "the hinterland"; Rieu, "the higher route") and came to Ephesus.

A commercial and religious center, Ephesus was situated in a fertile plain in the Roman province of Asia, near the mouth of the Cayster River. The site of the city, now a place of ruins, is near the coast of the Aegean Sea, thirty-five miles south-southeast of Izmir (Smyrna), Turkey. In Paul's day Ephesus was one of the greatest cities of the Roman world, boasting a population of nearly 500,000.

Ephesus was the residence of the Roman governor, and for all practical purposes the city was the capital of Asia. (It is questioned whether the capital of the province had been officially transferred to Ephesus in New Testament times.) Its economic importance derived from the fact that the city was situated on the great north-south road of western Asia Minor and was in position to control trade flowing into the interior of Asia Minor along the Meander and Lycus valleys.

Religiously, Ephesus was the center for the worship of Artemis (Diana), a fertility goddess represented in statuary as a grotesque, many-breasted figure. The temple of Artemis in Ephesus, considered one of the seven wonders of the ancient world, was 180 feet wide and 377 feet long. The roof was supported by 117 sixty-foot columns, each of which was six feet in diameter. The temple stood on a platform 239 feet wide, 418 feet long. The ritual of the temple services consisted in sacrifices and ceremonial prostitution. In addition to its cultic use, it served as a refuge for fugitives from justice and as a bank for treasures.

For a period of about a month in the spring of each year there were special religious festivals in Ephesus connected with the worship of Artemis. Devotees poured into the city from many other provinces to participate in these festivals.

A rival to Corinth in moral corruption, Ephesus was a center for the practice of sorcery and every form of black art. There are evidences that Ephesus offered the greatest challenge and opportunity for service which Paul had encountered (cf. 1 Cor. 16:9) and that here he met some of his severest opposition. In 1 Corinthians 15:32 he speaks of fighting with beasts in Ephesus; 2 Corinthians 1:8-10 seems to allude to a severe illness which the apostle suffered in Ephesus.

Paul had visited Ephesus briefly on his second missionary journey (18:19), and had left with a promise to return (18:21). The visit made during the third journey (present passage) lasted for approximately three years (cf. 20:31), a longer period than was spent in any other city to which the apostle's missionary work took him. It is possible that in Ephesus, as in Corinth, Paul made his home with Aquila and Priscilla (cf. 1 Cor. 16:19). Acts 20:20 implies that he ministered from house to house. Toward the end of the first century the apostle John was associated with the church at Ephesus (cf. Rev. 1-3).

1. *The contact with the ill-informed disciples of John the Baptist (vv. 1-7).* It is not said that these people were associated with Apollos. Had they been, he no doubt would have given them additional instruction after Aquila and Priscilla had given him a fuller understanding of the Gospel.

It is a question whether these twelve men were Christians. Bruce thinks this is "certainly to be inferred from the way in which Luke describes them as 'disciples'," explaining that "this is a term which he commonly uses for Christians" (p. 385). On the other hand, their answer to Paul's question (v. 2) and Paul's response to their answer (vv. 3, 4) implies that they had never been saved. Apollos, who had experienced John's baptism, was apparently not rebaptized, but these people were. It appears that they had been immersed without understanding the significance of the act (cf. v. 4).

Other matters for consideration in this paragraph concern its bearing on the doctrine of the Holy Spirit (vv. 2, 6), the ritual of the imposition of hands (v. 6), and speaking in tongues (v. 6). Limitations of space prohibit a detailed discussion, but the following observations may be made: (1) Paul's question (v. 2) assumes that the Spirit is normally received at conversion: "Did you receive the Holy Spirit when you believed?" (NIV) — not when you prayed, when you emptied yourself, etc., but *when you believed.* (The KJV rendering of this verse is incorrect.) (2) The laying on of hands, mentioned here, chapter 8, and chapter 9 as occurring in connection with the reception of the Spirit, seems to have been a symbolic act. It is never commanded or taught in the New Testament as a requisite for receiving the Spirit. (3) There is no way of knowing exactly what the speaking in tongues was, whether ecstatic speech (as in 1 Cor. 12; 13) or known languages (as at Pentecost).

2. *Paul's ministry in the synagogue (vv. 8, 9).* Earlier (cf. 18:20) Paul had met the Jews of Ephesus, and they had urged Paul to stay longer with them. Now, having returned, he preached fearlessly to them concerning the kingdom of God for a period of three months (v. 8). When some were hardened and refused to believe, "speaking evil of the Way" before the whole congregation, Paul turned from them and took with him those who had become disciples (v. 9).

3. *Paul's ministry in the lecture hall of Tyrannus (10-20).* The Ephesians did their heavy work in the morning hours and rested from about 11 A.M. to 4 P.M. Tyrannus, an Ephesian teacher, likely taught his classes during the morning hours, and in the afternoon, when the building was not in use, Paul was permitted to give daily addresses in the lecture room. One Greek text expressly states that Paul had use of the building from 11 A.M. to 4 P.M. This continued "for the space of two years," and during this time the Gospel spread throughout the province so that "all they that dwelt in Asia heard the word of the Lord" (v. 10, ASV). The churches of Colossae, Smyrna, Philadelphia, etc. may have come into being at this time.

Incidents singled out by Luke are (1) the "special miracles" (Goodspeed: "extraordinary wonders") wrought by Paul (vv. 11, 12), (2) the experience with the sons of Sceva[3] (vv. 13-16), (3) the public burning of the scrolls of those who practiced sorcery (vv. 17-20),[4] (4) the plan to visit Rome (vv. 21, 22), (5) and the riot of the silversmiths (vv. 23-41). The riot is described with considerable fullness: its leader (vv. 23, 24), its cause (vv. 25-27), its course (vv. 28-34), and the intervention of the town clerk (vv. 35-41).

Verse 23. "No small stir" is a figure of speech which means "a very great disturbance — a riot. "That way" is a reference to Christianity — considered as a course of life, a way of salvation (cf. 9:2; 18:25; 22:4; 24:14, 22).

Verse 24. "Demetrius" appears to have been a wealthy and influential person, probably head of the guild of silversmiths. "Silver shrines for Diana" literally means "silver temples of Artemis." Though Artemis, among the Romans, was identified with Diana

---

[3]Sceva is called "a chief priest." Blaiklock thinks he was head of a "course" of Levites; Hackett interprets the phrase to mean that Sceva was a priest of the higher class; Bruce conjectures that Sceva had given himself the title "chief priest of the Jews."

[4]Observe the summary given in verse 20, and compare it with other similar statements in Acts (6:7; 9:31; etc.).

(hence the use of the name "Diana" in KJV), the Ephesian Artemis had little but the name in common with the Roman Diana. The latter was thought of as a beautiful virgin huntress, but Artemis of the Ephesians was worshiped as the goddess of fertility in man, beast and nature. Artemis (Diana) was the patron goddess of the city of Ephesus, and a temple dedicated to her worship was located there. The trade of the city flourished upon the worship of Artemis and the flow of pilgrims which that worship attracted to the city. The "silver shrines" here mentioned were probably small models of the temple (possibly containing an image of Artemis) which were used for souvenirs, dedicatory gifts, and household idols. They may also have been worn as charms.

Verse 25. "By this craft we have our wealth" means "Our prosperity depends upon this work" (TCNT). The first concern of Demetrius and his associates was the threat to their livelihood created by the preaching and progress of the Gospel.

Verses 26, 27. Not only was their livelihood at stake; the majesty of the goddess Artemis, indeed the validity of their entire religion, was being challenged. (Read these verses in NEB.)

Verse 28. The goddess Artemis (Diana) was an object of worship throughout the Roman world, and "Great Artemis (Diana)" was the usual way of addressing her.

Verse 29. The riotous outburst of the silversmiths soon affected the entire populace, and a demonstration was staged in the city's open-air theater. This theater was a large circular enclosure excavated in the hillside. It had a diameter of no less than 495 feet and accommodated approximately 25,000 people.

"Gaius" was a rather common name in New Testament times (cf. Acts 20:4; 1 Cor. 1:14; 3 John 1). We therefore cannot be certain of the exact identity of the man mentioned here. On "Aristarchus" compare Acts 20:4; 27:2; Col. 4:10, 11; Philemon 24. Both of these men must have been rather recent converts, and it is worthy of note that they were soon busy at work as missionaries.

Verse 31. "The Asiarchs" (ASV) were the chief officers of Asia. Weymouth: "public officials"; NEB: "some of the dignitaries of the province."

Verse 35. The "town-clerk" kept the archives of the city, had charge of its money, and presided over its assemblies. In short, he was the most influential person of the city. Moffatt translates, "secretary of state." Bruce calls him "the executive officer who published the decrees of the civic assembly" and explains that as "the most important Ephesian official," he acted "as liaison officer between the civic administration and the Roman provincial administration" (p. 401).

The town clerk first told the mob they had been shouting a thing known by everyone (vv. 35, 36). Then he pointed out that there was no basis for charging the Christians with crime, and that if Demetrius and his followers had a charge to bring they should go through the legal procedures of the courts (vv. 37-39). He closed his speech with a reminder to the mob that by their rashness they had endanged the liberties allowed the city by Rome (v. 40). With this, "he dismissed the assembly" (v. 41).

In Ephesus the Gospel confronted idolatry, superstition, and vested economic interests. The opponents of Paul were well aware of the tremendous power of the Gospel and rightly saw it as a threat to the whole structure of their pagan society. Consequently they fought it with fierce intensity.

Let us learn from this that (1) the world in which the Gospel was first preached was in some respects much like ours — questioning, unbelieving, contemptuous, and hostile; (2) opposition to the Gospel always intensifies when vested interests are challenged; and (3) such opposition is no excuse for failure to present faithfully the claims of Christ.

4. *The work in Macedonia and Greece (20:1-3).* Soon after the visit in Ephesus, Paul sent for the disciples, spoke words of encouragement to them, and left for Macedonia (v. 1). Luke says little about Paul's ministry in Macedonia (v. 2), but the apostle may have stayed there for a prolonged period (perhaps about a year; cf. Bruce, pp. 404, 405). The Corinthian correspondence suggests that during this time Paul was gathering an offering for the poor Christians of Palestine. Also during this time he seems to have made a trip either up to or into Illyricum, a province north and west of Macedonia.

By "Greece" (v. 2) we are to understand the province of Achaia. Here (mainly in Corinth) the apostle spent three months. Bruce thinks they were the winter months of A.D. 56, 57; Hiebert, 57, 58. During this period Paul wrote his epistle to the Romans.

It seems to have been Paul's original plan to sail directly from Cenchrea to Syria, but learning that the Jews were plotting to kill him once he was on board the ship he changed his plans and instead returned to Macedonia to sail from there (v. 3).

5. *The journey to Jerusalem (20:4—21:6).* The missionaries traveled by way of Philippi to Troas (vv. 4-6). The seven men named in v. 4 were representatives from the churches from which Paul had gathered the offering for Palestine. From a study of 2 Corin-

thians 8; 9), one may assume that Titus also was among the group. It is strange that Luke has omitted his name from the list and that the name does not appear anywhere else in Acts. Ramsay accounts for this by assuming that Titus was Luke's brother, and that family modesty led him to avoid direct references to him in Acts.

We may assume that Luke rejoined Paul at Philippi (note "us," v. 5; "we," v. 6) and that these two remained briefly in Philippi while the seven men of verse 4 went on to Troas (cf. v. 5). After the Passover Paul and Luke sailed to Troas, where they spent seven days. The fact that the journey required five days (v. 6) suggests that there were strong head winds. Earlier, the trip from Troas to Neapolis had been made in two days (cf. 16:11, 12).

The incident concerning Eutychus, recorded in verses 7-12, occurred on the last day of the visit in Troas. Observe that it occurred on "the first day of the week" (v. 7). This is the first mention in Acts of "the first day" in connection with a service of worship.

(1) *From Troas to Miletus* (20:13-16). Luke (note "we," v. 13) and other members of the missionary party, in accordance with arrangements made by Paul, left by ship for Assos, a coastal town south of Troas. Paul, who remained behind in Troas (perhaps to give additional instructions, perhaps because he desired solitude, perhaps because he wanted to visit friends along the way), was to travel by land and meet them at Assos (v. 13). This all took place according to the plan, and Paul, boarding the ship, journeyed with his companions to Mitylene (v. 14). From Mitylene, the main city on the island of Lesbos, they touched at the islands of Chios and Samos and came in two days to Miletus, the southernmost of the Greek cities of Asia Minor. In Paul's time it was a relatively unimportant city of the province of Asia.

Luke writes that Paul, desirous of reaching Jerusalem before the day of Pentecost, "had determined to sail past Ephesus, that he might not have to spend time in Asia" (v. 16). Some think the language implies that Paul and his group were on a chartered ship and had control over its ports of call. Ramsay thinks the meaning is that they had a choice of two ships, one which stopped at Ephesus, another which stopped at Miletus.

(2) *Paul's message at Miletus* (20:17-35). From Miletus Paul sent to Ephesus for the elders of the Ephesian church. Upon their arrival at Miletus the apostle delivered the words recorded in verses 18-35. This is the only recorded speech of Paul which was delivered to Christians. It is mainly hortatory and contains numerous parallels to his epistles. From it we may infer that Paul's enemies in Asia had attempted to prejudice the minds of his converts against him.

The persons for whom this address was intended are called "elders" in verse 17, "bishops" in verse 28. In verse 28b their function is described by a verb whose root is the same as that for pastor or shepherd (cf. NIV).

The theme of the address is fidelity in the ministry. In many respects it is the most personal and most affectionate address which has come down to us from Paul. No analysis of it can do justice to it, but the following are the main lines of thought: Verses 18-21 set forth the example of the apostle's own ministry, calling attention to his lowliness of mind, compassion, hardships (v. 19), and his fidelity in preaching (vv. 20, 21; cf. vv. 26, 27). Verses 22-27 speak of his plans for the future. Verses 28-31 contain a charge for the Ephesian elders: to take heed to themselves (v. 28) and to shepherd the church (vv. 28-31). In verse 32 the apostle commends them to God, and in verses 33-35 reminds them again of his example.

Verses 36-38 describe the affectionate and tearful parting. "They all wept as they embraced him and kissed him. What grieved them most," Luke explains, "was his statement that they would never see his face again" (NIV).

(3) *From Miletus to Tyre* (21:1-6). In rapid fashion Luke narrates the journey to Tyre. The first stop was "Cos," an island about forty miles south of Miletus and famous as the birthplace of Hippocrates. The next stop was the island of "Rhodes," famous for its great lighthouse (the "Colossus of Rhodes") which was considered one of the seven wonders of the ancient world. Paul probably stopped at the city of Rhodes, on the northern tip of the island. "Patara" was a city on the coast of Lycia, a province just south of Asia. At this point the travelers changed ships and, passing within sight of the island of Cyprus[5] (visited on the first journey), sailed to Tyre, a Phoenician city which was now a part of Syria.

At Tyre, where the missionaries remained seven days, Paul was told by the believers that he should not go to Jerusalem (v. 4). The apostle apparently took their words, spoken "through the Spirit" (v. 4), as information and warning but not as a divine prohibition. All the disciples and their wives accompanied the missionaries out of the city, and after they knelt together in prayer on the beach, there was an affectionate farewell reminiscent of that at Miletus (vv. 5, 6).

(4) *From Tyre to Caesarea* (21:7-14). Completing the voyage, the party disembarked at Ptolemais (modern Acre or Akko). One

---

[5]"Leaving it on the left hand" (v. 3, ASV) means "passing to the south of it" (NIV).

of the oldest cities in the world, Ptolemais was located in what is now northern Israel on the tip of the bay which sweeps southward to Haifa. It afforded the best harbor on the Palestinian coast.

Caesarea, known also as Strato's Tower, had its beginning in the third century B.C. and passed under Roman control in 63 B.C. Herod the Great began the rebuilding of the city in 22 B.C., completed it twelve years later, and named it for Caesar Augustus. Herod made a harbor by dropping immense stones into the sea and constructing a breakwater two hundred feet wide. In A.D. 4 Caesarea became the Roman capital of Judea and the official residence of the procurator. The site of the city, located between Tel Aviv and Haifa, is marked today by the ruins of a Roman hippodrome, a Roman aqueduct with well-preserved arches and conduit, a Roman theater, various Crusader ruins, and so on.

At Caesarea the missionaries were entertained in the house of Philip, who is here described as "the evangelist, who was one of the seven", (cf. 6:5; 8:4-40). About twenty years separate this appearance of Philip and the last reference made to him (8:40). An "evangelist" was one especially gifted to proclaim the good news to those who were unevangelized.

Philip's "four unmarried daughters" (v. 9, NIV) were all prophetesses, which means that they had the gift of speaking for God utterances given them under the immediate inspiration of the Spirit.

Agabas (v. 10) is the same man who is mentioned in 11:28, where we are told of his predicting a famine which was to come upon Judea. Here, speaking in the Spirit, he assured Paul that imprisonment at the hands of the Jews awaited him in Jerusalem; on hearing this Luke (note "we," v. 12) and all the people present pleaded with Paul not to go. But Paul, in spite of the tears of his friends, was determined to go on. Gently pushing aside their loving arms, he replied, "Why are you weeping and breaking my heart? I am ready not only to be bound, but also to die in Jerusalem for the name of the Lord Jesus" (v. 13, NIV). Paul apparently interpreted the Spirit's warnings (here and at Tyre, v. 4) as intended not to deter him from going to Jerusalem but to prepare him for what awaited him there. He had an inward spiritual constraint which impelled him to go to Jerusalem whatever the cost (cf. 19:21; 20:22).

We have no way of knowing what there was which so peremptorily demanded Paul's presence in Jerusalem. He may have felt that, because of the hostility which the Jews had toward him it was important that he deliver in person the offering which he had been gathering for the poor of Jerusalem. Stalker thinks Paul may also "have been solicitous to procure from the apostles a message for his Gentile churches, giving an authoritative contradiction to the insinuations of his enemies as to the unapostolic character of his gospel. At all events there was some imperative call of duty summoning him, and, in spite of the fear of death and the tears of friends, he went forward to his fate" *(Life of Paul,* pp. 126, 127).

(5) *From Caesarea to Jerusalem* (21:15, 16). A few days later,[6] writes Luke, "we took up our carriages ['baggage,' ASV] and went up to Jerusalem" (v. 15). The word translated "we took up our carriages" means to equip, make ready (cf. RSV, Williams). Some understand it here to refer to equipping or saddling horses (Souter, *Lexicon;* Ramsay, *St. Paul the Traveller,* p. 302). Others think it refers to packing baggage. Moulton and Milligan interpret the word to mean "having furnished ourselves for the journey" *(Vocabulary of the Greek Testament,* p. 244). Hackett suggests there is a reference in the word to the offering being taken to Jerusalem, which he thinks consisted in part of food and clothes.

At Jerusalem, a distance of sixty-four miles from Caesarea, Paul and his party were brought by friends from Caesarea "to the home of Mnason" (v. 16a, NIV), described here as "a man from Cyprus and one of the early disciples" (v. 16b, NIV). Luke's mention of the fact that Mnason was an "early disciple" (i.e., one of the original Jerusalem disciples) leads some interpreters to suppose that Luke may have received some information from this man about the early days of Christianity (cf. Bruce, pp. 426, 427).

Upon his arrival in Jerusalem, Paul presented to the church the offering which he had gathered from afar (cf. Acts 24:17; Rom. 15:31).

FOR FURTHER STUDY

1. Read the account of the third missionary journey and make a list of all of Paul's companions in travel.

2. What were the sources and kinds of opposition encountered on this journey?

3. Use a map to trace the course of the third journey.

---

[6]Longenecker *(The Ministry and Message of Paul,* p. 78) writes that for a man in a hurry to get to Jerusalem, a delay of several days in Caesarea "appears somewhat strange and raises the question as to why there was a break in the journey here." After suggesting several possible explanations, he concludes that Paul's stay in Jerusalem was largely "a wait for the proper moment for entrance into Jerusalem." Paul's desire was to be in Jerusalem "on the day of Pentecost (Acts 20:16) — not just to arrive in Jerusalem as early as possible, but to arrive at what he believed to be the strategic moment."

4. Use a dictionary to study Elder and Bishop.

5. Why was Paul so eager to go to Jerusalem, in spite of warnings that harm awaited him there?

CHAPTER 8

Captivity of Paul

(Acts 21:17—28:31)

The section we are now to study covers a period of four or five years, beginning about A.D. 58 (Hiebert) or 59 (Ogg). The material is wholly concerned with the events leading up to the arrest of Paul and his subsequent imprisonment — in Jerusalem (21:17—23:35), in Caesarea (24:1—26:32), and in Rome (chs. 27; 28).

Stalker thinks that Paul by this time must have been nearly sixty years old. "For twenty years he had been engaged in almost superhuman labors. He had been traveling and preaching incessantly, and carrying on his heart a crushing weight of cares. His body had been worn with disease and mangled with punishments and abuse; and his hair must have been whitened, and his face furrowed with the lines of age. As yet, however, there were no signs of his body breaking down, and his spirit was still as keen as ever in its enthusiasm for the service of Christ" *(Life of Paul,* pp. 125, 126).

I. JERUSALEM (21:17—23:35).

The following matters are presented in reference to Paul's stay in Jerusalem: (1) his meeting with James and the elders of the Jerusalem church (21:17-26), (2) his seizure by the mob (21:27-40), (3) his defense (22:1—23:11), and (4) his removal to Caesarea (23:12-35).

1. *The meeting with James and the elders of the church (21:17-26).* Having arrived at Jerusalem, Paul was warmly welcomed by the brethren who were in sympathy with his work (v. 17). On the following day he and representatives of the Gentile churches met with James (the Lord's brother, cf. 15:13ff.) and the elders of the church in Jerusalem in a formal assembly (v. 18). At this meeting Paul described in detail *(Modern Language:* "recounted to them step by step," v. 19) all that God had done among the Gentiles

135

through his ministry. Upon hearing this, the entire assembly began praising God *(Amplified Bible:* "they adored and exalted and praised and thanked God," v. 20a). They did, however, express concern about the reactions of many Jewish believers to Paul's presence in Jerusalem. "You see," they said, "how many thousands of Jews have believed, and all of them are zealous for the law. They have been informed that you teach all the Jews who live among the Gentiles to turn away from Moses, telling them not to circumcise their children or live according to our customs" (vv. 20b, 21, NIV). The language implies that James and his associates did not believe this rumor, and that they are on the side of Paul. That Paul encouraged Timothy to submit to circumcision is an indication that the charge was false (cf. 16:3).

It appears that zeal for the law on the part of some within the Jerusalem church had intensified considerably since Paul's "famine visit" (11:30). Some conjecture that this was because many former Essenes, who had been accustomed to strict observance of the law, had joined the ranks of the Jerusalem church. James and the Jerusalem apostles are not reported to have favored this development, but there are indications that they had been hard-pressed to contain it.

The proposal which grew out of Paul's meeting with James and the elders is presented in verses 22-25. The essence of it was that Paul, in order to alleviate the fears which the malicious rumors about him were generating, should give evidence publicly of his respect for Jewish customs by joining in the (Nazarite) purification rites about to be performed by four Jewish Christians, and by paying their expenses. "Then everybody," they explained, "will know there is no truth in these reports about you, but that you yourself are living in obedience to the law" (v. 24, NIV). Then they reaffirmed the agreement reached at the Jerusalem council: "As for the Gentile believers, we have written to them our decision that they should abstain from food offered to idols, from blood, from the meat of strangled animals and from sexual immorality" (NIV).[1]

Verse 26 tells of Paul's response to their proposal: On the following day, he "took the men and purified himself with them" (NIV), giving notice at the temple when the period of purification would end and when the sacrifice for each of them would be made. This was an evidence of the apostle's willingness to go a "second

---

[1]That the ceremonial law was not to be imposed on Gentile believers was settled at the Jerusalem council (ch. 15); but it was not stipulated that it was wrong for Jewish Christians to continue to observe the law, if they chose to do so.

mile" to prevent serious trouble in the church; and since the thing he did was not a required ceremonial, it was in no way a compromise of his doctrine of salvation apart from the law (cf. 18:18; 1 Cor. 9:20). Evidently his action succeeded in averting a crisis, for the trouble which eventually occurred was instigated by unbelieving Jews.

2. *Paul's seizure by the mob (21:27-40).* When the seven days required for the purification were nearly over, fanatical Jews from the province of Asia, catching a glimpse of Paul at the Temple, stirred the crowd to a frenzy and seized him. They kept shouting, "Men of Israel, help us! This is the man who teaches all men everywhere against our people and our law and this place. And besides, he has brought Greeks into the temple area and defiled this holy place" (v. 28, NIV).[2] Luke explains that this latter charge was made because they had previously seen Trophimus the Ephesian in company with Paul in the city and had jumped to the (erroneous) conclusion that the apostle had taken him into the Temple (v. 29).

The entire city was thrown into confusion, "and people came running from all directions" (v. 30, NEB). Seizing Paul, they dragged him out of the inner precincts into the outer court of the Temple, and immediately the gates in the wall between the inner and outer courts were shut behind him (presumably by the temple guards).[3]

While his assailants were trying to kill the apostle, word reached "the chief captain of the band" (i.e., "the commander of the Roman troops," NIV)[4] that all Jerusalem was out of control ("in riot," Rieu). So he at once got together some officers and soldiers and swept down upon the rioters "at the double" (NEB). At the sight of the commander and his soldiers, the mob stopped beating Paul (vv. 31, 32).

At this point the commander went up to Paul, arrested him, and commanded that he be bound with a double chain ("handcuffed on both sides," Rieu; "shackled with two chains," NEB). Then he

[2]Gentiles were permitted in the outer court of the Temple, but there were signs posted in three languages warning them on pain of death not to enter the court of Israel.

[3]It was the responsibility of the temple guards (Levites) to prevent any disturbance within the Temple.

[4]The official title was "chiliarch," commander of a thousand soldiers. The guard which he commanded was stationed in the Tower (Fortress) of Antonio, which was at the northwest corner of the temple area. Built by Herod the Great, it served as a royal residence as well as quarters for the guard. Pilate's judgment hall was perhaps located in the Tower of Antonio (cf. John 18:20-40).

"began to inquire who he might be and what he had done" (v. 33b, Rieu). Some in the crowd shouted one accusation and some another, and since it was impossible to ascertain the facts, he ordered that Paul be taken into the barracks ("the Fort," Rieu; v. 34). But as Paul was going up the steps which led to the barracks, the violence of the mob became so fierce that he had to be carried by the soldiers. The mob, following right behind them, was yelling, "Kill him!" (vv. 35, 36).

Just as the soldiers were about to take Paul into the barracks, he asked the commander if he could say something to him (v. 37). The commander, surprised to hear Paul speaking Greek, asked, "Aren't you the Egyptian who some time ago stirred up a rebellion and led out into the desert four thousand cutthroats" (Gr., *sikarioi,* "dagger-men"; v. 38)? In reply, Paul assured him that he was a Jew of Tarsus, "a city of some note," TCNT ("not a bad city at all," Norlie), and courteously begged for permission to speak to the people (v. 39). The commander granted the request, and Paul, taking his stand on the steps, motioned for the attention of the people. At this, a great hush came over the mob, and Paul began his address, in the Hebrew (Aramaic) dialect (v. 40).

3. *Paul's defense (22:1—23:11).* The defense was in two stages: before the mob (22:1-29) and before the Sanhedrin (22:30—23:11). The former was an informal statement; the latter, part of an official hearing before the supreme council of the Jewish nation.

(1) *Defense before the mob* (22:1-29). Paul's defense took the form of a personal testimony regarding his religious experience, especially his sensitivity to the divine will. Throughout the address there runs an implied question: "How could I have done otherwise without being disobedient to God?"

Its substance. In verses 3-5 he recounts the prominent facts of his life before he became a Christian: his birth as a Jew ("a true-born Jew," NEB) in Tarsus; his training in Jerusalem at the feet of Gamaliel, according to the strict customs of the ancestral law; and his attitude toward Christianity ("the Way"). Verses 6-11 relate the story of his conversion, pointing up that it occurred while he was on a mission of persecution (vv. 5, 6) and was brought about by an appearance of the risen Lord (vv. 7-11). The point insisted on is that it was *God* who turned his life about. Verses 12-16 tell of the role of Ananias. Here Paul was careful to show that Ananias was a devout Jew, highly esteemed by all the Damascene Jews. The miracle (v. 13) performed by Ananias was a proof that God was with him, and his words communicated to Paul that God intended him to preach to *all men* (vv. 14, 15).[5] In verses 17-21 Paul tells of his commission, as reiterated in the vision at Jerusalem (cf. 9:26ff.). Three things are stressed: that God had commanded him to leave Jerusalem (v. 18), that he himself had protested (vv. 19, 20), and that God had pointedly told him to go to the Gentiles (v. 21).

Its outcome (vv. 22-29). The effects of Paul's speech are described in reference to the mob (vv. 22, 23), the commander of the Roman garrison (v. 24), and Paul (vv. 25-29). The mob is more enraged than ever. At the mention of the word "Gentiles" (v. 21), they could endure no more; "with a roar of disapproval they cried out, 'Away with such a fellow from the earth! He ought not to have been allowed to live' " (v. 22, Weymouth; NIV, "Rid the earth of him! He's not fit to live!"; NEB, "down with him! A scoundrel like that is better dead!" Rieu, "Wipe him off the face of the earth! Such a man isn't fit to live"). The commander was puzzled by it all, perhaps being unable to understand Paul because the latter spoke in Hebrew (Aramaic). Therefore when the Jews began to tear off their clothes and hurl dust into the air, he was determined to find out the reason for such a commotion. So, commanding that Paul be brought into the barracks, he directed that his soldiers beat the truth out of him (v. 24). Paul was then bound to the whipping post ("stretched . . . out with straps," Rotherham), but before the scourging[6] could begin the apostle asked the centurion who was in charge, "Is it legal for you to flog a Roman citizen who hasn't even been found guilty?" (v. 25, NIV).[7] On hearing this the centurion lost no time in going to the commander. "Do you know what you are doing?" he asked. "This man is a Roman citizen" (v. 26, TCNT). The commander, disturbed at this word, went to Paul and asked, "Are *you* a Roman citizen?" "Yes," replied Paul. Then the men who were to have flogged Paul imme-

---

[5]Verse 16 seems, on the surface to teach that baptism has saving efficacy. This verse, however, should be studied in light of the whole teaching of the New Testament. When this is done, one sees that baptism is only an outward expression of an inward experience. Sins are removed by the blood of Christ; baptism is a symbol or picture of that cleansing.

[6]The scourge, "a fearful instrument of torture" (Bruce, p. 445), consisted of leather thongs with pieces of metal or bone sewed in them. Men often died under the scourge; those who survived were usually crippled for life. At Philippi Paul had been beaten with rods (16:22), but the scourge was more brutal; Roman citizens, in fact, were legally exempt from it (cf. Bruce, p. 445).

[7]Two laws were about to be broken: (1) administering punishment to a Roman citizen without a trial and (2) submitting him to the scourge.

diately drew back; the commander also was alarmed, especially since he had bound him to the whipping post (vv. 27-29).[8]

(2) *Defense before the Sanhedrin* (22:30—23:11). The next day the commander of the Roman guard, having discovered that Paul was accused of some religious offense, ordered the Sanhedrin into session and brought Paul to the council chamber (located "on the western slope of the temple hill," Bruce, p. 447). The purpose of this hearing was to determine exactly what Paul had done, and whether it was an offense for which a Roman citizen could be legally punished.

When Paul was given permission to speak, he fixed his eyes on the Council and proceeded to give his defense. Three features of the passage should be observed: a. The interruption of the high priest.[9] So incensed was he by Paul's claim to have lived all his life in good conscience before God (v. 1) that he ordered those who stood beside the apostle to strike him on the mouth (v. 2). Paul's retort was quick and indignant: "God shall smite thee, thou whited wall" (v. 3; "you white-washed wall!!," TCNT; "you whited sepulcher," Montgomery).[10] Reprimanded by those who stood by him for reviling God's high priest, Paul replied, "I knew not, brethren, that he was high priest" (v. 5, ASV). This statement has given rise to considerable discussion, it being difficult to understand why Paul would not know that it was the high priest who ordered the smiting. Some have suggested that he was speaking in grave irony (cf. Lindsay, II, 123); others, that Paul may not have been looking in the direction of the high priest when the latter gave his order and so was unable to distinguish the exact source of the words. Still others have intimated that Paul's bad eyesight may have been the reason for his failure to recognize the high priest. Keep in mind that it was not a regular session of the Sanhedrin but one summoned by the Roman officer. The high priest, therefore, may not have been in his usual place, nor clad in his high-priestly robe. At any rate, Paul, who had been in Jerusalem for only brief and in-

---

[8]The reference to Paul's being "bound" (v. 29) is uncertain. Some take it to denote his being bound to the whipping post (v. 25); others, his being bound with two chains (cf. NEB).

[9]Bruce calls the high priest of this time (Ananias, son of Nedebaeus) "one of the most disgraceful profaners of the sacred office" (p. 449). Once during his high priesthood (A.D. 47-59) he was suspended and taken to Rome for trial. In A.D. 59, because of his notorious conduct, he was deposed. Ten years after that he was murdered by the Jews because of his pro-Roman sympathies.

[10]"The metaphor of the 'whited wall' suggests a tottering wall whose precarious condition has been disguised by a generous coat of whitewash" (Bruce, p. 451).

frequent visits for many years, would not have recognized the face of the high priest.

b. Paul's tactic to throw the council into confusion (v. 6). Realizing that his situation was hopeless, Paul decided to produce a division in the assembly. This he did by speaking in the interest of a truth (the resurrection of the dead) about which he knew his judges sharply disagreed. As a result, "a great uproar ensued" (v. 9a, TCNT; Rieu: "loud and confused shouting broke out"), and some of the scribes who belonged to the Pharisaic party sprang to their feet and declared that they found Paul guilty of no crime. "And what if," they said, "a spirit hath spoken to him, or an angel?" (v. 9b, ASV). The dissension by this time had become so violent that the Roman commander, fearful that Paul might be torn in pieces by them, ordered the troops to go down and rescue the apostle and bring him into the barracks (v. 10).

c. The vision of encouragement (v. 11; cf. the vision at Corinth, 18:9, 10), which came the night after the appearance before the Sanhedrin. The Lord, in the vision, encouraged Paul in his present distress and assured him that he would not die at this time but would bear witness at Rome. Incidentally, the words of the Lord imply his approval of Paul's visit to Jerusalem.

4. *Paul's removal from Jerusalem (23:12-35)*. The narrative concerns the following: (1) the plot against Paul's life (vv. 12-24), (2) the letter· of explanation to Felix (vv. 25-30), and (3) the trip to Caesarea (vv. 31-35).

a. The plot against the life of Paul was the immediate cause of the decision to transfer him from Jerusalem to Caesarea. The planning of the plot is described in verses 12-15. More than forty men (v. 13) conspired to kill him by ambush, binding themselves under a solemn oath that they would neither eat nor drink until he was dead. (They must have become rather hungry, for it was about nine years before the apostle was put to death!) That they could enlist the aid of the chief priests and the Sanhedrin is an indication of the moral and spiritual bankruptcy of the religious leaders of Israel at the time.

How the plot was foiled is told in verses 16-24. In brief, Paul's nephew learned of it and managed to get to Paul to inform him (vv. 16, 17), and then to the Roman commander (vv. 18-21). Several tantalizing questions emerge in reference to this incident: Who was this nephew? Where did he live? How old was he? How did he come by his information? Was he a Christian? As to his identity, all we know is that he was Paul's sister's son. The family could have lived in Jerusalem, but it has been suggested by some that they lived in Tarsus and that the young man had come to Jerusalem to study, as had his uncle Paul years before. We cannot know his exact age. The word used to describe him ("young man") is the same as that used to describe Paul in 7:58. Nor can we know how the young man obtained his information. One writer suggests that a Pharisee might have told him — as an act of kindness to Paul, a fellow Pharisee. Bruce thinks he may have been present when the plot was hatched. Verse 16, he says, might be translated: "But Paul's sister's son heard the plotting, having been present, and he entered into the fortress and reported it to Paul." The manner in which the young man is introduced implies that he was a Christian, but we cannot be certain of this.

The Roman commander, Claudius Lysias, acted promptly on the information given him by Paul's nephew (vv. 22-24). Believing the lad's story to be plausible, he arranged to send Paul by night under heavy escort to Caesarea. In all, 470 soldiers were assigned to the mission, two hundred infantrymen, seventy cavalrymen, and two hundred spearmen. The heavy guard was not for the purpose of restraining Paul from escape, but rather to protect him from those who might attempt an ambush on the way. When they arrived at Antipatris, a town about half way between Jerusalem and Caesarea, all but the cavalrymen returned to Jerusalem. At Caesarea, which was the Roman capital of Palestine, Paul would be under the responsibility of the governor.

b. The letter of explanation to Felix (vv. 25-30). It was a requirement of Roman law that a subordinate officer in reporting a case to his superior should send a written statement of the case. Accordingly, Claudius Lysias, the Roman commander in Jerusalem, sent a letter of explanation to the governor in Caesarea. Furneaux calls it "a dexterous mixture of truth and falsehood." Obviously, Claudius Lysias was attempting to put himself in a good light, and in doing so found it necessary to handle the truth loosely. Incidentally, he indicated, as did Felix and Festus later, that in his opinion Paul was innocent (v. 29).

c. The trip to Caesarea (vv. 31-35). The soldiers escorting Paul left Jerusalem about 9 P.M. (cf. v. 23) and by morning had reached Antipatris (vv. 31, 32), a distance of about thirty-five miles. Feeling they were now out of reach of the conspirators, the foot soldiers returned to Jerusalem, leaving the cavalrymen to escort Paul the remaining twenty-seven miles to Caesarea. Upon arriving in Caesarea, the military escort delivered the letter of Claudius Lysias to the governor and also handed over Paul to him (v. 33). After inquiring of Paul the province from which he came, the governor promised to give him a full hearing as soon as his accusers arrived (vv. 34, 35a). Then he gave orders that Paul was to be kept in custody in "Herod's judgment hall" (v. 35b). "Judgment hall" ("palace," ASV; "Government House," TCNT) comes from a Greek word *(praitorion)* which comes from the Latin *praetorium*. Used only here in Acts but five times in the gospels, it originally designated the general's quarters in a Roman army camp, but it came to be used of the official residence of the governor. It was called "Herod's" palace because Herod the Great built it as a residence for himself.

II. CAESAREA (24:1—26:32).

The date of Paul's arrival in Caesarea was about A.D. 58 (Hiebert; Ogg, 59; Haenchen, 55; Turner "Chronology, *"Hastings Bible Dictionary,* 56). Here he was confined to Herod's palace for at least two years (24:27), though he was given some freedom of movement within his confinement (cf. 24:23). Luke appears to have been in Caesarea during the period of Paul's imprisonment there (cf. "we," 27:1), and it is thought by some that his gospel was written at this time.

1. *Under the custody of Felix (24:1-27).* Felix, the eleventh procurator of Judea (A.D. 52-59), owed his advancement to this position to the influence which his brother Pallas exercised at the court of Claudius. Prior to his assumption of the office of procurator, he held an unimportant post in Samaria (A.D. 48-52). The years of his tenure as procurator were marked by increasing unrest throughout the province, and the ruthlessness with which he dealt with it only heightened the problem. He was notorious for his corrupt political life, and his private life was no better. Tacitus, who described Felix as cruel and lustful, wrote that he "exercised the power of a king with the spirit of a slave."

(1) *The trial before Felix* (vv. 1-23). "After five days" (i.e., five days after Paul's arrival at Caesarea),[11] Paul's accusers made their appearance. The delegation consisted of "Ananias the high priest" and "certain elders" (representing the Sanhedrin) and "an orator" ("attorney," Goodspeed; "spokesman," RSV) named "Tertullus" (v. 1a). Bruce thinks Tertullus, "whose name was a common one throughout the Roman world," was a Hellenistic Jew (p. 463). These "stated to the Governor the case against Paul" (v. 1b, Weymouth).

A summary of Tertullus' speech is given in verses 2-8. In it

---

[11]Some (e.g., Carver) think the meaning is five days after Paul's arrest in Jerusalem (cf. the "twelve days" of v. 11).

there is an introduction, marked by lavish flattery (vv. 2-4),[12] a statement of the charges against Paul (vv. 5, 6), and a conclusion (vv. 7, 8).

Mention is made of his being (1) "a pestilent fellow" (v. 5a; "public pest," TCNT; "troublemaker," NIV; "source of mischief," Weymouth; "veritable plague," *Modern Language*), a mover ["inciter," Montgomery; "organizer," Norlie] of sedition ["insurrections," ASV; "discord," NEB; "riots," NIV] among all the Jews" (v. 5b); (2) "a ringleader of the sect[13] of the Nazarenes" (v. 5c); and (3) a profaner of "the temple" (v. 6a; NIV, he "even tried to desecrate the temple"). These charges, it may be seen, range from the more general to the more particular.

Verse 9 reports that the Jews joined in the attack on Paul, brazenly affirming that all the charges preferred against Paul by Tertullus were true.

Paul's defense is given in verses 10-21. There is a brief introduction (v. 10b)[14] which is in marked contrast to the empty flattery used by Tertullian, followed by a statement concerning the charges (vv. 11-16) and an explanation of what really happened in Jerusalem (vv. 17-21).

Two of the charges the apostle denied, asserting that his accusers could not prove them (vv. 11-13), but he readily admitted to being a follower of the Way which his accusers contemptuously called "a sect" (vv. 14ff.). He indicated that in so doing he was rendering service (worship) to the God whom his Jewish ancestors had served (v. 14a); affirmed his belief in everything in agreement with the Jewish Scriptures (v. 14b); asserted that he shared the hope of the resurrection professed by his accusers (v. 15); and protested that, with this hope before him, he was doing his utmost to keep his conscience clear before God (v. 16).

Having answered the charges, Paul proceeded to explain just what did happen in Jerusalem at the time of his arrest (vv. 17-21). After an absence of several years, he had come "to bring my people gifts for the poor and to present offerings" (v. 17, NIV).[15] He was

---

[12]Felix was one of the worst governors the Jews ever had, but Tertullus characterizes him as a political reformer!

[13]The use of this word shows that the Jerusalem Jews still thought of Christianity as a Jewish party.

[14]Paul simply acknowledges that Felix had been governor for many years (six or seven at the time); this is about all that could be said honestly. Paul's statement implies that Felix, by virtue of his several years in the office, would be acquainted with Jewish customs.

[15]Bruce calls this "the clearest reference in Acts — indeed, ... the only refer-

ceremonially clean when they found him in the Temple, with no crowd about him and no uproar (v. 18). Alluding to the absence of the Asian Jews who had created the disturbance in Jerusalem (v. 19), the apostle challenged his opponents to state what crime the Sanhedrin had found in him when he stood before them in Jerusalem (vv. 20, 21).

Felix adjourned the proceedings, using as his excuse that he desired to confer with the Roman commander (Claudius Lysias) (v. 23). Paul was put back under guard, but the centurion was charged to allow him a measure of freedom and permit his friends to minister to his needs (v. 23). So far as we know, Lysias, who had previously given his opinion that Paul was innocent, never came to Caesarea.

(2) *The preaching of Paul to Felix* (vv. 24-27). Luke tells, in verses 24 and 25, of a specific occasion when Paul was summoned by Felix to speak to him "concerning the faith in Christ Jesus." With the governor at the time was Drusilla, youngest daughter of Herod Agrippa I (cf. ch. 12) and third wife of Felix. Her first marriage, which occurred before she was sixteen years old, was to the king of Emesa, an insignificant state in Syria. Felix had persuaded her to leave her husband. She was now only about twenty. One Greek text represents Drusilla as the one who desired the interview with Paul.

Paul's discourse, in which "he reasoned ['argued,' RSV] of righteousness ['justice,' Weymouth; 'morality,' Moffatt], temperance ['self-control,' ASV; 'the mastery of passions,' *Modern Language*], and judgment to come," was especially appropriate for the audience. "Felix trembled ['was terrified,' ASV; 'became alarmed,' NEB], and answered ['interrupted,' TCNT], Go thy way for this time ['That will do for the present,' NEB]; when I have a convenient season ['when I can spare the time,' *Modern Language*], I will call for thee."

In verse 26 Luke explains that after this Paul was frequently summoned to appear before Felix for conversation. Greedy soul that he was, the governor hoped that he might extract a bribe from the apostle. This continued for two years, at the end of which Felix

---

ence — to the collection which Paul had organized in the Gentile churches as a gift to the Jewish Christians of Jerusalem" (p. 470).

Opinions vary as to the meaning of "offerings." Some (e.g., Hackett, Lumby) conjecture that the reference is to the sacrifice connected with the vow mentioned in 21:26. Others (e.g., Knowling) think it possible that the allusion is to an offering (perhaps a thank-offering) connected with the Feast of Pentecost. Bruce, Lenski, and others understand "offerings" to refer to the same thing as "alms." This, perhaps, is the best explanation though the words are carefully separated in the text.

was deposed by Nero at the request of the Jews and was succeeded by Porcius Festus. It was customary, when there was a change of governors, to release prisoners who were unconvicted. Festus, however, desiring to curry favor with the Jews, "left Paul bound" (v. 27).[16]

2. *Under the custody of Festus (25:1—26:32).* Festus, who became governor about A.D. 60, died in office two years later. Though he seems to have been a man of nobler character than Felix, Paul fared no better under him.

(1) *The trial before Festus* (25:1-12). The arrangements for the trial are recounted in verses 1-5. Three days after becoming governor, Festus went up to Jerusalem to confer with the leaders of the Jewish people. Thinking it an opportune time, they presented their charges against Paul, asking as a favor that the governor have Paul brought to Jerusalem (vv. 1-3a). Their intention, Luke explains, was to ambush the apostle and kill him (v. 3b). Festus, however, did not accede to their request; instead, he told them that he was to be in Jerusalem only a short time and that they should send representatives (men of authority, their leaders) to accompany him to Caesarea (vv. 4, 5a). There they could charge the apostle with whatever crime he had committed (v. 5b).

The trial is reported in verses 6-12. Festus left Jerusalem for Caesarea after eight or ten days. On the day after his arrival, he took his place on the judge's bench and sent for Paul (v. 6). As soon as the prisoner arrived the Jews surrounded him and presented a variety of grave charges, none of which they could prove (v. 7). (This time, the Jews presented their own case, not employing the services of an attorney [such as Tertullus, cf. 24:1].) Paul, in defense, maintained that he had committed no crime against Jewish law, against the Temple, or against Caesar (v. 8). Festus, wishing to win the favor of the Jews, interrupted the apostle and asked if he would be willing to go to Jerusalem and be put on trial there (before the Jewish Sanhedrin) in his presence (v. 9). Paul, having endured two years of the procrastinations of Felix and sensing that justice under Festus was just as remote, made a dramatic move: "No," he replied, "I take my stand at Caesar's tribunal, where I have a right to be tried. I have committed no crime against the Jews, as you yourself know well enough. If I have broken the law,

---

[16]Many questions are suggested by Luke's brief account of Paul's imprisonment under Felix. For example: What led Felix to think that Paul was a man of means, able to pay him money? What happened to Silas? He was not, so far as we know, imprisoned with Paul; and he appears only one more time in the New Testament (1 Peter 5:12). What were Timothy and Luke doing during this time?

or have committed some crime for which I ought to die, I do not ask for a reprieve; but if there is no truth in the charges against me, it is not for anyone to hand me over as a sop to the Jews. I make my appeal to Caesar" (vv. 10, 11). Festus, after conferring with his advisors, replied, "You have appealed to Caesar. To Caesar you will go!" (v. 12, NIV). The governor was doubtless surprised by Paul's move and was perhaps distressed. It would not look good for him to have this, his first case as governor, taken from his jurisdiction and submitted to the emperor. However, as a Roman citizen, Paul was acting completely within his rights.

(2) *The hearing before Herod* (25:13—26:32). A short time after the trial, "king Agrippa and Bernice came unto Caesarea to salute ['pay official respects,' Williams; 'welcome,' *Modern Language*] Festus" (25:13). This was Herod Agrippa II, son of Herod Agrippa I (cf. ch. 12), and half brother of Drusilla (the wife of Felix). Because of his youthful age (seventeen years) at the time of his father's death, Agrippa II was not appointed to succeed him as king of Judea. Four years later (A.D. 48), however, he was made king of Chalcis, a small province in northern Palestine. Then in A.D. 53 he was permitted to exchange this kingdom for the tetrarchies formerly ruled by Philip and Lysanius. In addition, he was given control over the temple and had the right to appoint high priests. After three years, Nero added to Agrippa's domain several cities and villages around the Sea of Galilee. His capital was at Caesarea Philippi, the name of which he changed to Neronius. Agrippa was educated in Rome and was in thorough sympathy with the policies of Rome. When Jerusalem fell in A.D. 70, he returned to Rome and, about A.D. 100, died there.

Bernice, who was Agrippa's sister, was first married to her uncle, but upon his death, she went to Rome to live with her brother Agrippa. To keep down scandalous talk, she married a second time. However, when Agrippa was made a king, she left her husband and went again to live with Agrippa as his wife. Later she became mistress to both Vespasian and Titus.

The king and Bernice prolonged their stay for many days; and Festus, knowing that it would be necessary for him to send a written report of Paul's case when the prisoner was dispatched to Rome, seized this as an opportunity to get at the root of the matter (cf. 25:26, 27). Agrippa, as a part Jew, was familiar with Jewish law and customs, and would know how to explain the charges against Paul (v. 14a).

In 25:14b-21 Luke records *the explanation* made by Festus to Agrippa, and in verse 22a reports that Agrippa confessed to a frequent desire to hear Paul (cf. Knox, Phillips). "To morrow," said Festus, "thou shalt hear him" (v. 22b).

In 25:23 Luke describes the setting. Agrippa and Bernice with regal splendor entered the audience room, accompanied by "high ranking officers ['military commanders,' Moffatt] and the leading men of the city" (NIV). Then Festus gave the order for Paul to be brought in. The latter, when he arrived, was in chains (cf. 26:29). Festus' introduction of Paul, along with a brief summary of his case, is given in 25:24-27.

Paul's testimony (26:1-29), which is reported with great fullness, is a masterpiece of eloquence. In substance, it is very similar to the speech made in Jerusalem on the steps of the Tower of Antonio (ch. 22). There is a brief *introduction* (vv. 2, 3), in which Paul expresses his pleasure at being given the opportunity of speaking, commends the king on his knowledge of Jewish affairs, and asks for a patient hearing. This is followed by *the address* (vv. 4-23). In it he recounts the story of his life up to his conversion (vv. 4-11), making mention of his early Jewish training (v. 4), his strict religious life (v. 5),[17] and his persecution of the church (vv. 9-11);[18] recalls in graphic language his conversion and commission (vv. 12-21), telling of the "heavenly vision" on the road to Damascus (vv. 12-18) and of his response to it (vv. 19-21); and affirms his innocence (vv. 22, 23), declaring that God is on his side (v. 22a) and that what he preaches is the fulfillment of what Moses and the prophets predicted (vv. 22b, 23).

The message closes with *an appeal* to Agrippa (vv. 24-29). Paul's enthusiasm and his reference to the resurrection (v. 23) were too much for Festus. Shouting at the top of his voice, he exclaimed: "Paul, you are raving mad" (v. 24a, Montgomery). "Your great learning is driving you insane" (v. 24b, NIV). Paul made a courteous reply to Festus (v. 25) and turned again to Agrippa to press home the claims of Christ (vv. 26, 27). Opinions vary as to the exact meaning of Agrippa's reply (v. 28). Whether he spoke seriously or in sarcasm we cannot know. Most interpreters, however, seem to think his words betray insincerity and cynicism. Lake and Cadbury, for instance, contend that " 'Christian' in the mouth of Agrippa can only be interpreted as a sneer" (p. 322).[19] Hackett

[17]Verses 6-8 are a kind of parenthesis showing how utterly inconsistent the Jews were in bringing their charge against Paul.
[18]He explains that this was done out of a sense of duty (v. 9) and that he was acting as representative and agent of the chief priests (v. 10; cf. v. 12). The intensity of his hatred of the Christian movement was shown by the fact that he pursued Christians even to foreign cities (v. 11).
[19]They offer two possible translations: (1) "You rapidly persuade me to make

thinks Agrippa was moved by Paul's earnest manner but attempted "to conceal his emotion under the form of a jest" (p. 289). Bruce is of the opinion that Agrippa was embarrassed by Paul's appeal. "He may have listened with interest enough, and possibly Paul hoped that the apparent interest might develop into something more. . . . But Agrippa was not minded even to appear to lend support to Paul's case. . . . So he turned Paul's appeal aside with a smile" (pp. 495, 496).

At the close of Paul's appeal, the audience withdrew and, after discussing the matter, concluded that Paul had done nothing to deserve either death or bonds. Had he not appealed to Caesar, said Agrippa, he might have been set free (vv. 30-32).

III. ROME (27:1—28:31).

Once it was decided that Paul was to be sent to Italy, he was handed over, along with some other prisoners, to a centurion (cf. discussion of 10:1) named Julius (27:1). The troops which were commanded by Julius were called the "Augustan band" (ASV; "Imperial regiment," Moffatt), "Augustan" being "a title of honour very frequently bestowed upon auxiliary troops" (Schurer, as quoted by Carter and Earle, p. 392).

The story narrated in chapters 27 and 28 revolves around (1) Paul's journey to Rome (27:1—28:16) and (2) his experiences in Rome (28:17-31).

1. *The journey to Rome (27:1—28:16).* The account of the journey, which Bruce calls "a small classic in its own right" (p. 498), is given from the point of view of an eyewitness (note the recurrence of "we," "us"). Aristarchus of Thessalonica, in addition to Luke, was permitted to accompany Paul on this trip (v. 2). Ramsay thinks both Luke and Aristarchus traveled as Paul's slaves "not merely performing the duties of slaves . . . but actually passing as slaves" *(St. Paul the Traveller,* p. 316). There may have been other friends of Paul on the voyage, but they are not mentioned.

The journey was begun in the early autumn of A.D. 60 and concluded in the spring of 61 (Hiebert). (Ogg puts the departure in 61 and the arrival in 62.) It was considered hazardous to sail the Mediterranean after the middle of September, and from the middle of November until March, navigation was generally suspended.

The journey required travel by sea and by land. In all, three different ships were used: one boarded at Caesarea (27:2), another at Myra (27:5, 6), and still another at Melita (28:1). Luke gives

---

a Christian" — that is, to help you to convert Festus. (2) "You rapidly persuade me to play the Christian" (p. 323).

special attention to the disastrous storm encountered, the behavior of Paul in the crisis, and the three-month stay on the island of Melita (Malta). A classic treatment of Luke's narrative is James Smith's *The Voyage and Shipwreck of St. Paul,* first published in 1848 but, since the exhaustion of the fourth edition (published in 1880), is out of print.

The trip to Rome was in four stages: (1) *Stage one: Caesarea to Myra* (27:2-5). Apparently a ship going directly to Rome was not available. They therefore boarded a ship which was engaged in coastal trade and claimed Adramyttium (in northwest Asia Minor) as its home port (v. 2). Julius must have been certain that at one of its ports of call they could book passage on a ship bound for Rome. They touched at Sidon, where Julius, as a kindness to Paul, permitted him to visit friends in the city and get any care he needed (v. 3); sailed along the south coast of the island of Cyprus because the winds were against them (v. 4); then, heading in a north-westerly direction, they came to Myra (a city in the province of Lycia) (v. 5).

(2) *Stage two: Myra to Fair Havens* (27:6-8). At Myra the centurion found a grain ship (cf. 27:38) from Alexandria which was sailing for Italy, and put those in his company on board. They sailed slowly for many days and, with the wind checking their progress, came with difficulty to a point off Cnidus, a peninsula which projects from the coast of Asia Minor just north of Rhodes (v. 6). The wind not permitting them to hold their course, they then sailed along the south coast of Crete, availing themselves of the protection of the island (v. 7). It was still with difficulty that they moved, but eventually they came to Fair Havens, a place about equidistant between the east and west ends of Crete.

(3) *Stage three: Fair Havens to Malta* (27:9—28:10). By the time the ship had reached Fair Havens, winter was at hand; for, as Luke explains, "the Fast" (the Day of Atonement) was already past (v. 9). Ramsay thinks a ship's council was held and that Paul, recognized as an experienced traveler, was invited to attend. The apostle, realizing the danger involved in continuing the voyage at this time, admonished that they pass the winter in Fair Havens and set sail again in the spring (v. 10). He had already been in three shipwrecks (2 Cor. 11:25), and was wary. The centurion, however, was more influenced by "the master ['pilot,' Weymouth; 'captain,' TCNT] and the owner of the ship" than by what Paul said (v. 11). Moreover, since the haven was ill-adapted for winter quarters the majority favored sailing on, hoping to reach the more commodious harbor of Phoenix (modern Phineka). Luke describes it as "a har-

bor in Crete, facing both southwest and northwest" (v. 12, NIV).

a. The storm (27:13-26). When a gentle southerly breeze began to blow, they decided they could easily make it to Phoenix; "so they weighed anchor and sailed along the shore of Crete" (v. 13, NIV). However, they had hardly left Fair Havens when they were beset by a violent northeast wind coming down from Crete (v. 14). They were forced to let the ship, caught in the grip of the wind, give way and be driven before it (v. 15).

Three dangers faced the beleaguered voyagers: (1) the loss of the small boat being towed behind them (v. 16), (2) the destruction of their own ship (hence the bracing of the ship by means of cables around its hull, v. 17a), and (3) the being cast upon "the Syrtis" (v. 17b; "the great sandbank near Africa," Beck; "the Syrtis quicksands," Norlie). "The Syrtis" was the name of two quicksands between Carthage and Cyrenaica. To guard against being cast upon these quicksands, they either "lowered the mainsail" (v. 17b, NEB) or "let down the sea anchor" (NASB).

So violently were they tossed by the storm that the next day they began to throw the cargo overboard (v. 18). On the following day, when the situation was becoming increasingly desperate, "they threw out the ship's tackle ['the spare tackle,' Rieu] with their own hands" (v. 19, TCNT). (This, of course, was to lighten the ship and decrease the danger of careening or listing.)" Then, when for many days neither sun nor stars were visible,[20] their hopes of coming through alive began to fade" (v. 20, NEB).

It was then, when the men had gone a long time without food, that Paul addressed them. His words contained both rebuke (v. 21) and encouragement (vv. 22-26).

b. The shipwreck (27:27-44). The storm had continued for two weeks (v. 27), and Paul had become the real commander of the ship. He aborted a cowardly attempt of the sailors to desert the ship (vv. 27-32), and then encouraged everyone on board (276 all told) to eat and be hopeful (vv. 33-38).

When daylight came, they caught sight of a bay with a sandy shore and "decided to run the ship aground if they could" (v. 39, NIV). They cut loose the anchors, dropping them in the sea; spread out the mainsail to catch the wind; and headed for the shore (v. 40). Unfortunately, "they found themselves caught between cross-currents" (NEB), and they ran aground (v. 41a). "The bow stuck fast, and . . . the stern was broken to pieces by the pounding of the surf" (v. 41b, NIV).

---

[20]Since ancient ships had neither sextant or compass, there was no way to determine directions when the sun and stars were obscured.

At this point the soldiers decided to kill all the prisoners, but the centurion forbade it in order to save Paul (vv. 42, 43a). He ordered those who could swim to jump overboard first and make their way to land, and the rest should follow on pieces of wreckage (vv. 43b, 44a). "And so it came to pass, that they escaped all safe to land" (v. 44b).

c. The refuge on the island of Malta (28:1-10). The shores on which the voyagers found safety were discovered to be those of the island of Malta, and three months were spent here before they continued on to Rome. Luke's narrative takes note of three things relative to the visit on this island: (1) the hospitality of the inhabitants (v. 2), who were probably of Phoenician origin; (2) Paul's recovery from the viper's bite (vv. 3-6); and (3) the healing of the father of Publius[21] and many others (vv. 7-10).

(4) *Stage four: Malta to Rome* (28:11-16). After spending the three months of winter on Malta, the shipwrecked voyagers, laden with gifts from the natives, boarded a ship which had wintered in the island. It was another Alexandrian ship (cf. 27:6), and it bore "the figurehead of the twin gods Castor and Pollux" (v. 11, NIV; Beck: "It had in front a figure of the Twin Sons of Zeus"; Montgomery: "Its name was 'The Twin Brothers'"; Norlie: "It was called the Dioscuri, after the twin brothers Castor and Pollux"). These two gods were regarded as the special protectors of sailors, their constellation, Gemini, being "considered a sign of good fortune in a storm" (Bruce, pp. 525, 526).

The ship made its way (perhaps in a single day) to Syracuse (on the southeastern coast of Sicily), where it docked for three days (v. 12). From there the mariners "made a circuit" (v. 13a, ASV; "circled round," Lamsa; "worked to windward," TCNT; "weighed anchor," Goodspeed) and reached Rhegium, on the southwestern tip of the Italian peninsula. On the next day a south wind began to blow, and this took them through the strait separating Italy and Sicily. On the day following they arrived at Puteoli (modern Puzzuoli), about 125 miles south of Rome in the Bay of Naples (v. 13b). In New Testament times this was the principal harbor south of Rome and was the port at which Egyptian grain ships regularly unloaded.

At Puteoli Paul and his companions found some fellow-believers[22]

---

[21]Publius is called "the chief man" of the island. The TCNT translates it "the Governor"; Rieu, "the chieftan"; Knox, "the leading citizen"; NEB, "the chief magistrate." A literal rendering is "the first man." Bruce thinks it was probably an official title.

[22]The presence of Christians at Puteoli is an indication of two things: (1) the

and were urged by them to remain for a week (v. 14a). (Some interpreters [e.g., Carver] think it probable that Julius the centurion left a soldier with Paul and that he himself went on to Rome with the other prisoners. Others [e.g., Bruce] suppose that the centurion had official business in Puteoli which required a week, and that Paul during this time was permitted to enjoy the hospitality of his friends [cf. 27:3]). "In this way," Luke adds, "we finally reached Rome" (v. 14b, Williams).

But before telling of the experiences in Rome, Paul goes back to tell of one incident which occurred between Puteoli and Rome. A short distance out of Puteoli the party reached the Appian Way, which would take them into Rome. The brethren at Rome, Luke explains, had "heard of us" — perhaps the Christians at Puteoli sent word about Paul's arrival in their city — and "came to meet us as far as The Market of Appius and The Three Taverns" (v. 15a, ASV). The former place ("Market Town," Beck), which Blaiklock describes as "a busy little trading town" (Cities of the New Testament, p. 83), was about forty-three miles from Rome; the latter ("Three Shops," Blaiklock, ibid.) was a village (or a stopping place along the road) ten miles nearer Rome. We are to understand that some of the believers from Rome went as far as The Market, others stopped and waited at The Three Taverns. Their purpose was to welcome Paul and escort him to the city. When Paul caught sight of them, "he gave thanks to God and took renewed courage" (v. 15b, Norlie).

When at length they entered the imperial city, Paul, manacled by a chain (cf. v. 20) to a soldier, was permitted to live as a private resident (v. 16). His great ambition to visit the capital (cf. Rom. 1:10-15; 15:23; Acts 19:21) was at last fulfilled, but he came not as a traveling evangelist (as he had hoped) but as a prisoner of Caesar awaiting trial.

2. *The Experiences in Rome (28:17-31)*. When Paul arrived in Rome, the city was already eight centuries old. Blaiklock thinks that even then there may have been "the suggestion of age and ruin in wall, road, and garden" but the city herself was "at the height of her imperial power" (Cities of the New Testament, p. 83). Nero, who about the time of Paul's arrival killed his own mother, was the emperor.

Toward the beginning of the Christian era Pompey did much to beautify and adorn Rome, but it was Augustus, first of the emperors, who could boast that he "had found the city built of brick

---

extent to which the Gospel had spread all over the empire and (2) the fact that Acts records only a small part of the story.

and left it built of marble." Rome, like Corinth, was strategically situated for commerce, and it inevitably attracted people from far and near. Probably by the time of Augustus the city had already reached a population of more than a million, and it was (as Blaiklock says) "a motley, cosmopolitan multitude" (p. 86). Juvenal, at the turn of the first century, wrote of "the misery, poverty, and inhumanity of the slum-ridden city, and the cruel inequities between its inordinately rich and its shockingly poor" (Blaiklock, p. 86). In the last book of the Bible Rome, likened to Babylon, is described as "the great prostitute who corrupted the earth by her adulteries" (Rev. 19:2, NIV).

> She has become a home for demons
> and a haunt for every evil spirit,
> a haunt for every unclean and detestable bird.
> For all the nations have drunk
> the maddening wine of her adulteries.
> The kings of the earth committed adultery with her,
> and the merchants of the earth grew rich from
> her excessive luxuries (Rev. 18:2, 3, NIV).

We do not know when or how the Christian community came into being in Rome, though many conjectures have been made. We do know that visitors from Rome were among those present in Jerusalem on the day of Pentecost (Acts 2:10), and it is not improbable that some of these were converted under Peter's preaching and took their new-found faith back to Rome. At any rate, about A.D. 57, when Paul wrote his epistle to the Romans, there was already a well-established church there, and the apostle could speak of their faith as being "reported all over the world" (Rom. 1:8, NIV). Bruce thinks the Roman church may well have been "one of the earliest . . . to be founded outside Palestine" (p. 531).

The account of Paul's experiences in Rome focuses on three matters:

(1) *His conference with the local Jewish leaders* (vv. 17-22). The meeting, which was requested by the apostle, occurred three days after his arrival in the city (v. 17a, cf. v. 20); its purpose was to explain the circumstances of his imprisonment (vv. 17b, 18) and the real reason for his presence in Rome (vv. 19, 20). The answer of the Jewish leaders, in which they denied all knowledge of Paul's case, is somewhat surprising (v. 21). It is quite possible that they spoke truthfully, but it is also possible that they professed ignorance of the case simply because they did not wish to become too deeply involved in it. They did, however, express a willingness to hear Paul's story (v. 22a), adding that it was known to them

that Christianity ("this sect") was denounced everywhere (v. 22b).

(2) *His preaching to a large gathering of Jews* (vv. 23-28).[23] Having arranged with Paul a day, a large group of the Jews came to his place of residence to be informed of his views (v. 23a). The apostle talked to them all day ("from morning till evening," vs. 23b), explaining and declaring the kingdom (reign) of God and attempting to "convince them about Jesus, by arguments drawn from the Law of Moses and from the Prophets" (v. 23b, TCNT). The reaction was mixed: "some believed . . . and some [apparently the majority] disbelieved" (v. 24, ASV). Unable to agree among themselves, they parted — but not before Paul had made a final statement. Citing Isaiah 6:9, 10, a passage in which Isaiah was warned that his people would not heed his message (vv. 26, 27), the apostle announced with a note of solemn finality that "God's salvation has been sent to the Gentiles, and they will listen" (v. 28, NIV).

(3) *His confinement in the city* (vv. 30, 31). Luke intimates that Paul's trial was delayed, and that during this time he remained in Rome as a prisoner. For "two whole years" he lived "in his own hired house" (v. 30a; "in a house which he rented for himself" TCNT; "at his own expense" (NIV), preaching to them the kingdom (reign) of God and teaching them about the Lord Jesus "with all boldness" (v. 31b, ASV; "utmost freedom," Phillips; "openly," Goodspeed) and "without hindrance" (Rotherham; "none forbiding him," ASV; "unmolested," TCNT). The Romans apparently did not consider the Gospel to be subversive, and the preaching of it was not deemed illegal.

These verses (30, 31) describe what traditionally has been called Paul's "first Roman imprisonment," the suggestion being that at the end of the two-year confinement in Rome the apostle was released. During the period of the first imprisonment he wrote Colossians, Ephesians, Philemon, and Philippians, and those letters should be read for supplementary information about Paul's activities, plans, and fellow-workers. The first three (Colossians, Ephesians, and Philemon) were written at about the same time, were carried by the same messenger (Tychicus), and were dispatched to the same part of the world (Asia). Philippians was probably the last of the four to be written.

It is widely held that Paul, after his supposed release and while engaged in further missionary endeavor, wrote letters to Timothy (First Epistle) and Titus. About the year A.D. 67, the theory states,

---

[23]Verse 29 (KJV) is lacking in the best Greek manuscripts.

Paul was arrested on orders from Nero and returned to Rome. On this occasion he was placed in the dungeon; from it he wrote his "last will and testament," the Second Epistle to Timothy. Shortly thereafter he was executed by the Roman authorities.

FOR FURTHER STUDY

1. Use a dictionary to study Centurion; Chief Captain *(chiliarch)*; and Tower of Antonio.

2. Why did Luke in writing Acts concentrate on the work of Paul so exclusively? Why did he not, in the latter part of his book, tell anything about the work of Peter or of Barnabas? Why did he make no reference to the work of most of the apostles?

3. Why does the Book of Acts close so abruptly, without even telling of the disposition of Paul's case?

Bibliography

Barclay, William, *The Acts of the Apostles* in "The Daily Study Bible" (Philadelphia: The Westminster Press, n.d.).

Blaiklock, E. M., *Cities of the New Testament* (Westwood, New Jersey: Fleming H. Revell Co.).

Blaiklock, E. M., *The Acts of the Apostles* in "The Tyndale New Testament Commentaries" (Grand Rapids: Wm. B. Eerdmans Publishing Company, 1959).

Bruce, F. F., *Commentary on the Book of Acts* in "The New International Commentary on the New Testament" (Grand Rapids: Wm. B. Eerdmans Publishing Company, 1956).

Bruner, Frederick Dale, *A Theology of the Holy Spirit* (Grand Rapids: Wm. B. Eerdmans, 1970).

Carter, Charles W. and Earle, Ralph, *The Acts of the Apostles* (Grand Rapids: Zondervan Publishing House, 1973).

Carver, William Owen, *The Acts of the Apostles* (Nashville: Broadman Press, 1916).

Hackett, Horatio B., *A Commentary on the Acts of the Apostles* in "An American Commentary on the New Testament" (Philadelphia: The American Baptist Publication Society, n.d.).

Knowling, R. J., *The Acts of the Apostles* in "The Expositor's Greek Testament" (Grand Rapids: Wm. B. Erdmans Publishing Company, n.d.).

Lake, Kirsopp and Cadbury, Henry J., *The Beginning of Christianity: Part I. The Acts of the Apostles* (Vol. IV, English Translation and Commentary) (London: Macmillan and Co., Ltd., 1933).

Lindsay, Thomas M., *The Acts of the Apostles* in "Handbooks for Bible Classes" (Edinburgh: T. & T. Clark, n.d.).

Longenecker, Richard, *The Ministry and Message of Paul* (Grand Rapids: Zondervan Publishing House, 1971).

Munck, Johannes, *The Acts of the Apostles* in "The Anchor Bible" (Garden City, N.Y.: Doubleday & Co., Inc., 1967).

Rackham, Richard B., *Acts of the Apostles* (Grand Rapids: Baker Book House, 1964) .

Ramsay, W. M., *St. Paul the Traveller and the Roman Citizen* (Grand Rapids: Baker Book House, reprint edition 1949).

Robertson, A. T., *The Acts of the Apostles,* Vol. III in "Word Pictures in the New Testament" (New York: Richard R. Smith, Inc., 1930).

Scroggie, W. Graham, *The Acts of the Apostles* in "The Study Hour Series" (New York: Harper & Brothers, n.d.).

Smith, Robert H., *Acts* in "Concordia Commentary" (St. Louis: Concordia Publishing House, 1970).

Stalker, James, *The Life of St. Paul* (New York: Fleming H. Revell Co., 1912).

Stifler, J. M., *An Introduction to the Study of the Acts of the Apostles* (New York: Fleming H. Revell Co., 1892).

Walker, Thomas, *The Acts of the Apostles* (Chicago: Moody Press, reprint edition 1965).

Winn, Albert C., *The Acts of the Apostles* in "The Layman's Bible Commentary" (Richmond: John Knox Press, 1960).

All Scriptures, unless otherwise identified, are quoted from the King James Version. Other translations referred to are as follows:

Goodspeed, Edgar J., *The New Testament: An Early American Translation* (Chicago: The University of Chicago Press, 1951).

Moffatt, James, *The New Testament: A New Translation* (New York: Harper and Brothers, 1950).

Montgomery, Helen Barrett, *The New Testament in Modern English* (Valley Forge: Judson Press, n.d.).

New American Standard Bible (Nashville: Broadman Press, 1960). Referred to in the Study Guide as NASB.

New International Version: New Testament (Grand Rapids: Zondervan Bible Publishers, 1973). Referred to in the Study Guide as NIV.

Norlie, Olaf M., *The New Testament: A New Translation* (Grand Rapids: Zondervan Publishing House, 1961).

Phillips, J .B., *The New Testament in Modern English* (New York: The Macmillan Company, 1962).

Rieu, C. H., *The Acts of the Apostles* (Harmondsworth, Middlesex: Penguin Books, Ltd., n.d.).

Rotherham, J. B., *The Emphasized Bible* (Grand Rapids: Kregel Publications, reprint edition 1967).

BIBLIOGRAPHY

The Modern Language Bible. The New Berkeley Version (Grand Rapids: Zondervan Publishing House, 1959).

The New English Bible (Oxford and Cambridge: University Press, 1965). Referred to in the Study Guide as NEB.

The Holy Bible: Revised Standard Version (New York: National Council of Churches in Christ, 1952). Referred to in the Study Guide as RSV.

The Holy Bible: American Standard Edition (New York: Thomas Nelson and Sons, 1929). Referred to in the Study Guide as ASV.

The Twentieth Century New Testament: A Translation into Modern English (Chicago: Moody Press, n.d.). Referred to in the Study Guide as TCNT.

Weymouth, Richard Francis, *The New Testament in Modern Speech*. Newly revised by James Alexander Robertson (New York: Harper and Brothers, n.d.).

Williams, Charles B., *The New Testament: A Private Translation in the Language of the People* (Chicago: Moody Press, 1949).